Feb. 25, 2001

To my new friend Lita —
I have travelled the world, and I think Alaska is the best. You can give joy wherever you are, and you are doing that. I hope you will find Alaska to be your permanent home!!

Fondly,

Lorene C. Harrison

Mostly Music

The Story of Lorene C. Harrison
Alaska's Cultural Pioneer

As Told to and Written by
Dianne Barske

Publication Consultants

PO Box 221974 Anchorage, Alaska 99522-1974

ISBN 1-888125-61-6

Library of Congress Catalog card Number: 99-067478

Copyright 1999 by Lorene Cuthbertson Harrison
— First Edition —

All rights reserved, including the right of reproduction in any form, or by any mechanical or electronic means including photocopying or recording, or by any information storage or retrieval system, in whole or in part in any form, and in any case not without the written permission of the author and publisher.

— Drawings of hats through the decades by Dianne Barske —

Manufactured in the United States of America.

Dedication

I share this history and these stories for my family, to whom this book is dedicated.
Lorene Cuthbertson Harrison

Author's Preface

Here's a little story. Prepare to laugh." How many times during the past four years have my Monday afternoons begun that way? I'd be sitting on Lorene's bed in her room in the Anchorage Pioneers' Home. She is sitting across from me, perched on a stack of pillows on her easy chair, looking pretty and fashionable.

"No more stories," I'd say after all those years. "Don't do another thing! Don't remember another thing! Your life's story is already encyclopedic. We'll have volumes - not a book."

We'd shared many laughs and quite a few tears over those years as I scribbled my notes, collecting the stories of this amazing woman and her 95 full years.

"Don't postpone joy," she'd tell me, and overall her life has been brimming with gladness. That's the path she has chosen. She has chosen to collect friends and to dwell on life's joyful moments.

"I wouldn't trade my life for any other," she says, even when remembering its more difficult moments.

She has done so much — in so many ways — to add to life in her community, Anchorage, Alaska. If she'd only focused her energies in one area, the task of writing her life's story would have been much less daunting.

As an indication of her varied contributions, there was the dilemma of choosing one title for her biography. Should it focus on hats and her millinery business and perhaps be called "Above All, A Hat"? Or should it focus on her television and radio shows and be called "Lorene's Scrapbook," as they were called? Should it relate to her role as the "founding mother" of so many of the musical arts organizations in this town? Ultimately it was music that won out — but not to the exclusion of her many other contributions. Thus, the title "Mostly Music" was chosen with the subtitle, referring to her "cultural pioneering," hopefully measuring up to much of what Lorene has done.

She's also a mother, grandmother, and great-grandmother. She's been a business owner, opening The Hat Box, long before it was common for a woman to assume this role, a community volunteer and founder of our first public kindergarten, a pageant chaperone, a world traveler — and a friend — to me and countless others.

Although I'd heard of Lorene Harrison almost from the moment I arrived in Anchorage with my family in 1975, it was at an opening of a show of my paintings back in 1979 that I first met Lorene personally. That moment is recorded in the photograph here, as we are both visiting with Anthony Paratore, a high school classmate of mine (Belmont High School, Belmont, Massachusetts, class of 1962), who had come with his brother, Joseph, as a piano duo under the auspices of the Anchorage Concert Association. Lorene was hostess for them as she was for so many others.

Life has a way of weaving circles around us sometimes, in curious and delightful ways. Twenty years after that photo, I feel honored to have come to know Lorene so well that we often finish each other's sentences. Obviously, I had no idea upon that first meeting that one day many years later I would be attempting to tell all that this woman

Here I am, back in 1979, at the opening of one of my art shows Downtown. I am visiting with high school classmate, Anthony Paratore, (Belmont High School, Belmont, MA - class of 1962!) here with his brother, Joseph, to perform in concert for the Anchorage Concert Association. And there is Lorene, smiling as usual, the hostess for the Paratores. Who could have known how our paths would overlap once again, some 20 years later?

has done to brighten her corner of the world. Her story needs to be told. She is a most remarkable woman. If music is joy, and I believe it is, if friendship is joy, and I know it is, then she has spread joy far and wide.

Dianne Barske

Foreword

This is a warm and lovely story of a lady and a legend. Or, to be more precise, it is the story of Lorene Harrison, a lady who became a legend as she helped shape the growth of a great American city over a period of more than 70 years.

The city is Anchorage, Alaska – now a modern metropolis of more than 260,000 residents. But it was home to only 3,000 people when she arrived on August 27, 1928 – hired at $180 a month to teach music and home economics at the town's only public school.

She was 23 years old at the time, embarking on what was a great adventure for a young woman who had grown up in rural Kansas. But from the day she arrived to become one of Anchorage's six high school teachers, she felt right at home in what she quickly realized was a vibrant community confident of its future.

It was the beginning of a great love affair. Lorene had come to what she later called "the greatest place on the face of the earth," where she found a life overflowing with "activity, creativity, love and fulfillment."

She lost no time in thrusting Anchorage into an exciting new world of culture and the arts. By September, just weeks after she had first set foot in her new home on the edge of the territorial wilderness, she had organized a high school choir. By mid-December, her high school students were performing in Anchorage's first operetta – described by a newspaper reviewer as "one of the most pleasing entertainments ever staged" in a town that then was only 13 years old.
It was the start of great things to

come under her energetic leadership. Other choirs and glee clubs, public concerts and stage productions, musical comedies and wartime community songfests at the USO, followed as the years rolled by.

She became a hostess of great fame, entertaining in her home the visiting artists and performers who came to Alaska at her invitation – many of whom, caught up by Lorene's enthusiasm, were captured by the spirit of the growing city. With her encouragement, they helped spread the word about Anchorage's emerging role as a center for the arts.

Her energy and talents, however, were not limited to music and the arts. For decades before and after statehood, Lorene was involved in a host of activities that placed her at the center of Anchorage's business and social life. This story recounts it all – in a marvelous retelling of how Anchorage grew, and in an unmatched recollection of those who were part of it all.

For those who have lived in Anchorage for a long time, Lorene Harrison's story brings to mind the names and places and events that made this city the great cosmopolitan center it has become. For newcomers to Alaska, the story of her life is a lively history lesson on how the state's largest city came to be what it is now.

As recounted in these pages, Elmer Rasmuson, a banker, philanthropist and a former mayor of Anchorage who also is worthy of being called an Alaska legend, once saluted Lorene Harrison – to use his words – for her industry, her accomplishments, her dreams, her vitality, her warmheartedness and her bright countenance.

She is, he said, an inspiration to all who know her.

The truth is, thank goodness, that after seven decades of service and after more than 90 years of joyful life, almost everyone in Anchorage knows Lorene Harrison. And even those few who don't are recipients of the great things she has accomplished.

"The City of Anchorage is a better place because of you," Elmer Rasmuson told her in his special tribute.

He speaks for all of us.

William J. Tobin
Anchorage, Alaska
June 1999

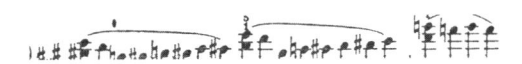

The Beginning of What Follows

Lorene's mother and father (in the 1940s) – Matthew Cuthbertson and Margaret Ellen ("Ella") Dunlap Cuthbertson.

Lorene standing with brother Will (Dr. William ALexander Cuthbertson, chiropractor) and sister Nina Marie Wyatt — 1962.

Lorene's brother Will's two sons and a daughter – (left to right) Bill Cuthbertson, Louise Frederick, Dr. Jim Cuthbertson. This photo was taken at a reunion in Hawaii in 1994. (Will's oldest son, Don Cuthbertson, died earlier.)

Lorene's sister Nina's three sons and their wives (left to right) Bob Wyatt, Jr. and Elda, Bill Wyatt and Fran, Dick Wyatt and Anna Lou. The photo was taken in 1997 at a family reunion in Sterling, Kansas.

Mostly Music

Lorene, far right, poses with daughters, Pegge, far left, and Carol Anne in the 1940s, in front of their Anchorage apartment on I Street. Lorene had made all the dresses, "probably for the girls' piano recital," she recalls.

The trio through the years — This was taken at the wedding of Carol Anne's daughter, Romney, in 1986.

And then in 1996 — "We seem to be sharing a good joke," Lorene says.

Again the trio gathered in 1989.

A recent photo (above) of Lorene's daughter Pegge and her husband, Joe Veilbig, in their yard in northern California.

Lorene's grandson (above), Eric Harrison Vielbig, and his wife Melody.

Lorene's grandson, Earl Veilbig, in 1992. He is holding his four-month-old son, Steven. This photo was taken before Earl's death in a drowning accident.

Lorene's great grandson (below), Steven, at age 5.

Grandson Earl's family—wife Sharon and son Steven.

Mostly Music

A recent photo (left) of Lorene's daughter Carol Anne and her husband, Bob Dodd, in their Anchorage home.

Granddaughter Kelli and her husband, Paul Watt, and greatgrandchildren, Shawn and Emili.

Granddaughter Diane Dodd (above) and Jeff Hermanson.

Grandson Ed Dodd, his wife Kari, and Lorene's great grandson, Jack.

Granddaughter Romney Ortland and her husband Stephen and Lorene's great grandchildren (left to right) Remy, Tanner and Davis.

Carol Anne's children (right), "the Dodd grandchildren who call me 'Grandma Hat,'" Lorene comments. Left to right: Kelli, Diane, Romney, and Ed.

Romney's wedding (1986) with sister Kelli, half-sister Tracey, the bride Romney, sister Diane, and brother Ed in back (below).

"And the flowers" – Entryway to Dodd's front door, Anchorage (below).

"The Flock" – Grandson Ed with Lorene's great grandsons in daughter Carol Anne's Anchorage backyard.

14

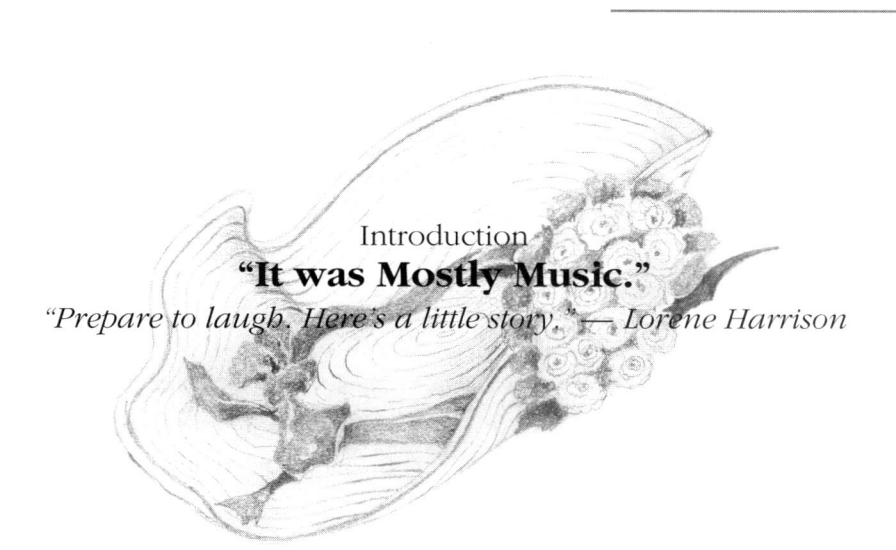

Introduction
"It was Mostly Music."
"Prepare to laugh. Here's a little story." — Lorene Harrison

Lorene Harrison has long known she holds in her memory a large part of the Anchorage cultural arts history, covering the past seven decades. Follow Anchorage arts organizations back to their roots and you will often find the name, Lorene Harrison. In fact, in October of 1996 at the fiftieth anniversary celebration of the Anchorage Concert Chorus (previously known as the Anchorage Community Chorus), she was introduced as "The Mother of Alaska's Musical Arts." The late Robert Atwood, who had been a publisher of the Anchorage Times, called her "something like the Queen Mother of the arts" in Anchorage.

Many years ago, Lorene began her story as a book, intending to share what she knows and her love of the place she first came to call home back in 1928 – Anchorage, Alaska. She states, "I was surely guided by a kind and wise Creator to this, the greatest place on the face of the earth, in my estimation. My life has been one of activity, creativity, and fulfillment. What more could one desire?"

Sitting down with pen and paper to record memories from that full life, a monumental task, to be sure, Lorene wrote, "I would like to write of some of my experiences for my six grandchildren — and perhaps others might also find them exciting or inspiring. I have not accumulated a great deal of money, but I have accumulated a great many friends — all over the world. I would not trade my life for any other that I know."

And then life's ongoing activities got in the way. Lorene is now 94, and she has been active and involved right up to the present day. "When I came here, I knew this was where I belonged. I saw a vital, young

Anne Lorene Cuthbertson, age 2
Sterling, Kansas, 1907

community with so much still to be done. They needed me, and I loved doing what they needed me for. It was mostly music."

As her story unfolds, something like a symphony, music is the recurring theme, but there are many other elements, variations on a theme, woven into its patterns. She was busy.

She never did get her autobiography written. And so her book has taken a different form. It is Lorene's story as told in countless visits with Dianne Barske over the course of the last three years, from her room in the Anchorage Pioneers' Home.

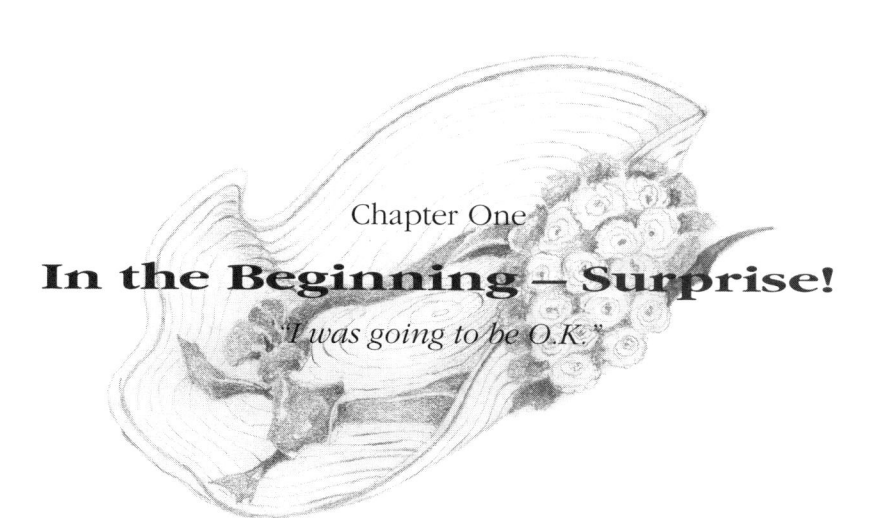

Chapter One
In the Beginning – Surprise!
"I was going to be O.K."

The very beginning of Lorene Harrison's story comes from those early autobiographical handwritten notes. These, then, are the words she intended as her book's beginning

My full name is Anne Lorene Cuthbertson Harrison. In the fall of 1904, my mother, then 43 years old, was having some "stomach trouble," so my father, then 52, sent her from the farm near Girard, Kansas, to Excelsior Springs, Missouri, for a rest and relaxation. Their 21-year-old son, Will, and Nina, the 15-year-old daughter, could ably help their father with the farm chores.

On March 7, 1905, mother's "stomach trouble" ended – I was born! So many times through the years my parents mentioned that I had surprised them when I came into the world, and never ceased giving them occasional shocks.

One critical shock component of Lorene's birth was the fact that she was a girl. Before she was born, her parents had been convinced that she would be a boy. Indeed, her mother and father had her name picked out, Orville Kenneth, so that her initials would be O.K. The plan was that O.K. would work the family farm, cultivating its fields as a young lad in the southeast corner of Kansas.

Lorene states that in adjusting to this surprise, her father changed his plans and "within the year sold the farm and we moved to the small college town of Sterling, Kansas. Sterling is in the center of Kansas and almost in the center of the entire United States, in its heartland." It was a town of about

3,000 people when Lorene was growing up there. At the time of Lorene's birth, brother Will was studying at Sterling College and sister Nina was attending high school, staying with friends in the town of Girard, traveling home to the farm by horse and buggy on the weekends.

Lorene, age 3, Sterling, Kansas — 1908. Lorene says, "Maybe this is my first hat!"

The Sterling Years

Lorene would spend her "growing up" years in Sterling, and the fact that her musical talent sprouted early and strong should not be so surprising when you look at her heritage, her roots. Her mother and father were both musicians. Her mother, Margaret Ellen Dunlap, of Irish descent, had played the pump organ. She had traveled by covered wagon with her parents at the age of two from Ohio to Kansas. Her father, Matthew Cuthbertson, born in Illinois, had played the violin and led a choir. Her grandfather had played the fiddle. Her father's side of the family was Scottish. There had been 11 children in his family; Matthew was next-to-the-youngest. As a boy of 17, he had traveled by covered wagon to Kansas with two of his older brothers.

In Sterling, Lorene's father would eventually buy a "soda pop" factory, spending his work days involved in making grape and orange soda pop and sarsparilla.

Lorene remembers her father as being the more mild mannered of her parents; her mother was the disciplinarian. Lorene admits that as a child she often let an adventurous and lively streak lead her into mischief. It would be her mother who tried to pull her back and keep her more in line. "She was not beyond sending me out into the yard to fetch my own switch. That left a stinging impression on me when my adventures had gone too far."

One of her earliest memories reflects her father's strong interest

Lorene Harrison

in her education. "He was very well self-educated and did lots of reading. He was president of the congregation at the Sterling Presbyterian Church and noted as a master of Robert's Rules of Order. Early Sunday mornings were a special time for the two of us. When I was about six years old, my mother would get up and get the breakfast, while I climbed in bed beside my daddy and he'd teach me something. He always had something planned for me to learn, sometimes spelling words and vocabulary. I remember the first word he shared with me for spelling and meaning — 'incomprehensibility.' He'd break it down into syllables and we'd go at it together until I had it right. Then he had me learn the books of the Bible — first the Old Testament books and then the New Testament." To this day, some 88 years later, Lorene can still spill out the names of the books of both testaments in rapid order.

"I can picture my father sitting at his old Oliver typewriter, working on some poetry. He was a published poet." Shortly after her grandparents sold their farm near Pittsburg, Kansas, her mother's parents, the Dunlaps, moved to Sterling and lived with the family there. Lorene remembers her mother spending much time caring for them.

Her father's spelling lessons took. "I was always a good speller," she states simply. Known as a stand-

Lorene's home in Sterling, Kansas, where she spent her first 19 years – "It was a wonderful home. I spent hours playing in the apricot tree in the back yard."

out in school spelling bees, Lorene still grimaces when recalling her "terrible mistake" in eighth grade. "I was up till the very last round. Then I got the word 'kimono,' and I missed it. That was a heart-breaker. I replaced the last 'o' with an 'a'."

The incident suggests an ability that has stayed with Lorene into her 90s,

Lorene at age 7 — "I am with the beautiful doll my sister, Nina, gave me that year. I still have her. Her name is Marceille."

Kanza Camp Fire Group – Sterling, Kansas — 1920. "Camp Fire was one of the most important parts of my Sterling childhood."

the ability to bring back names and dates and details from her life, sometimes from over 85 years back. Her life's tapestry, the events and people woven into it, are rich and important to her; she has forgotten little. If she stops and dwells long enough on a name or date, closing her eyes and thinking hard, she can draw it back, like pulling out the earliest threads of her life. "Let me think," she'll say. "I can get that name; it will come to me," she'll state, and startle even herself. Out will pop the name of someone she knew in the most cursory of ways — a substitute teacher, a store clerk — someone she has not thought of in decades.

One of the most important threads to her early life in Sterling is her membership in Camp Fire then known as Camp Fire Girls. She was involved in the organization almost from the day it was founded in 1915. "One of the first national Camp Fire groups was right in Sterling, Kansas. Our group was called the Kanza Camp Fire group, the name given to it from the New York Camp Fire headquarters. Camp Fire was to be such an important part of my life. There were 12 of us in the group; we were sixth graders."

Then, as if it were yesterday, Lorene rattles off the Camp Fire Oath of the Wood Gathers, the first of three degrees of the Camp Fire organization. "Seek beauty, give service, pursue knowledge, be trustworthy, hold onto health, glorify work, and be happy." The oath seems to be a kind of herald, a road map for the course Lorene's life would take. Her Camp Fire name is even more a personal harbinger. She was given the Indian name "Minowe," which means "Magic Voice."

Meetings centered around songs, beadwork and other crafts, and the making of their own costumes. "Our costumes were made of a heavy fabric, sort of like a linen, which we decorated with beads. We all had headbands with beadwork. Beads were earned; they were a token of honor."

The 12 members of Kanza also planned and went on hikes. "I remember one hike in particular. We went to Hannoncrat Grove at the edge of town, built our campfire, and made our chowder. We had just settled down to our meal, when we discovered that some cows observing our activities did not like us there. Each summer, we

Lorene with Marjorie McGarey in their Camp Fire dresses, made by the girls. Lorene's kitty, Caliban, stands nearby. Lorene's Camp Fire name was Minowe, meaning "Magic Voice."

went on a week's camping trip. Our fathers would drive us in their cars to the camp site. We'd bring along folding cots and our bedding and have a wonderful time."

Music entered her life through church as well as Camp Fire. Radio did not play a musical role in her elementary school years. Radio was a peculiarity, a novelty introduced into Sterling when she was in the seventh grade. "Radio was such a new idea that we actually had a field trip for my physics class to go see the first radio in Sterling. It was at the big mill. My teacher wanted us to see this marvelous new invention."

The "Terrible Trio" meets again – as adults. Marjorie, Lorene, and Florence.

Just as exciting was the Chautauqua, a kind of huge entertainment and educational road show in tents, that traveled throughout the country in the summers from 1903 to 1930. Sterling was on the Chautauqua route each summer. "We thought this was big stuff — not hometown stuff," Lorene states. "Most everybody went. There was usually a lecture on some topic, then music — both instrumental and vocal. Chautauqua was one of my first exposures to music when I was little, along with music at church and school." As the popularity of radio took hold, the popularity of these traveling road shows faded out.

It was through close childhood friends that perhaps Lorene's greatest joy in music came as a young girl. "Florence Currier, Marjorie McGarey and I were called 'the terrible trio.' We were very creative — not always very constructive! Florence played the violin. She played very well. Her violin teacher came each week from the big neighboring town of Hutchinson with 18,000 people, and Florence was one of his best students. Marjorie sang, and both Florence and I would play for her. I sang too and played piano for the trio. We were all eighth graders when we got our trio together."

Marjorie was the only daughter of a Sterling preacher. In 1909, Lorene's father had built the family home just one block from the preacher's home, on a lot in the same block as the home of the Sterling College president. When the family had first moved to Sterling shortly after Lorene was born, they had rented a home for three years, directly across from the college. There was never a time that the college did not play an important part in Lorene's life and the life of her family.

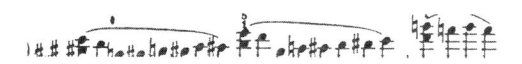

But the real appeal of the family's permanent home location was its nearness to friends. "Marjorie was so close that we could yodel back and forth to each other. We'd yodel each morning to let each other know when we were heading off to school. I would sometimes eat dinner with her family, and particularly remember a meal of 'pork and bings.' I came home to my mother and insisted that she make a meal of 'pork and bings' for me, like Marjorie's mother. My mother was quick enough to realize that I must mean pork and beans."

Lorene calls herself "never a really super student," although she always liked school. "I liked school and loved friends. I've always been a people person." She adds, "My grade cards have all been saved — mostly there were A's and B's, but physics and math drew some C's."

Formal music lessons began for Lorene in the third grade, when she started taking piano lessons. Voice lessons through the college began when Lorene was 14. It was then a school of approximately 500 students. "My mother kept a diary of my piano lessons. In it, she noted that each lesson cost 50 cents. Mrs. Davis, my piano teacher, drove her horse and buggy to her students' homes. Sometimes I wasn't completely ready for her. There were times when I didn't want to practice. I'd rather be tree climbing, swimming, biking. I loved my bicycle. In those days, I would

Marjorie McGarey Wilson, and Lorene, some 70 years later. "When this photo was taken, Majorie was living in Arizona and had become nearly blind. We had been lifelong friends, visiting on the phone several times a year."

have been known as a 'tomboy.'

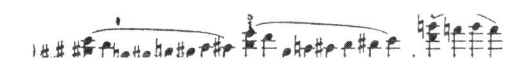

"There were many more boys than girls in our neighborhood. I would race the boys, pumping hard down the block on my bicycle. Or I'd bike out to my friend Bertha Matthews' home. She lived on a farm, and I loved to ride out on the country roads, three miles to her home. We slid down haystacks, and her family let me milk a cow. I remember squirting some of the milk directly into their cat's mouth.

Flossie English and Lorene, about 1918. "We're wearing Flossie's brother's overalls, much better than skirts for climbing trees."

"We'd go swimming and diving at the local outdoor pool. I was as good at swimming as any of the boys. I got my highest Camp Fire honors for swimming and diving. I loved swimming under water; I already had good breath control." It is tempting to label this as childhood vocal training for her later musical career.

But Lorene seems, even today, to have an easier time focusing on her youthful outdoor antics rather than on her childhood music lessons. Her attention moves quickly back to outdoor enterprises. "Our home had a huge apricot tree in the backyard, and colonnades at the back of the house. I could stand on the colonnade, throw my feet up into the apricot tree and then climb on up. I spent a great deal of time up in that tree. One of my favorite things to do was hunt for birds' nests in the branches."

She was often joined by another childhood friend, Flossie English, who lived only one house away from the Cuthbertsons. "Flossie was another tomboy. Girls didn't wear pants when we were growing up, and skirts can truly interfere with tree climbing skills. So we wore Flossie's brother's bib overalls. That worked."

Trees weren't the only things Lorene and Flossie climbed. There were the grape trellises in the backyard. They'd swing hand-over-hand from one trellis to another, like children on monkey bars today. They spent countless hours in a tree house in the apricot tree. And there was that all-too-tempting roof on the Cuthbertson two-story home.

"I remember one afternoon when I was 12 and my mother had gone off to a meeting of the missionary society. Flossie and I climbed to the top of the house. We were sitting side-by-side up by the chimney when my mother came home. What to do? Though she later told me that she had been scared to pieces, she thought a moment, and then told us calmly, 'I've been to the store. I've got some things you'd like.' She paused and started to go in the house as though all was well. 'You can have some when you come down.' With that she tempted us safely off the roof."

More "life on the wild side" was encouraged by Flossie's older brother and his friend. They had taken a liking to smoking the wild grape vine. "It was long and thin, like a string of spaghetti. Flossie and I decided, without much tempting on the boys' part, that we were ready to be wild right along with them." It was a very short-lived experiment. "It tasted terrible — just awful. I couldn't see any pleasure in that!" So ended childhood smoking for Lorene and Flossie.

More serious memories related to danger flicker back when Lorene recalls how the family home was invaded by robbers more than once. "Sterling attracted transients — hoboes, we called them back then. We were heading into the Depression years. They would come into town on the train and sometimes ask for work. My mother tried to have some work saved for them. She would give them meals on the back porch.

"One night someone got into our home through a small window over the kitchen sink. It might well have been one of these hoboes. I think we were spared much damage by the fact that my parents had added a bedroom and bath off the kitchen for my grandparents to live in. We think my grandparents frightened the intruders away when they heard a noise and got up. Regardless, the event left me very frightened. I would call out to my mother at night, telling her I needed her to get into bed with me."

Another time word that someone was breaking into homes in Sterling had spread through Lorene's neighborhood. "We were going to church one Sunday morning. On an impulse, my mother and I decided to hide our money from our purses under the rug. Someone did break in, but our money was safe under the rug."

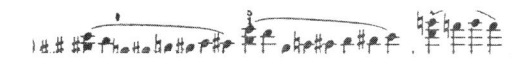

A love for pets as well as love for people played a part in Lorene's youth. "I had a darling little white rat named Ratta Rex, a male. Marjorie had the mate, a female. We loved to play with them and show them off. One evening, my parents were having a good-sized party in our home, 25 or 30 people sitting around on folding chairs we'd borrowed. My brother Will loved to play tricks and couldn't resist this big audience. Marjorie and I had brought our rats out, to show them off in their cages. I

The Cuthbertson cats, at least two of them, Fluffy and Caliban, at the front door of their Sterling, Kansas home. "There were 26 more cats in the barn — and two horses."

imagine people were trying to seem politely interested.

"Suddenly the lights went out. My brother had shut them off. Then he bellowed, 'The rats are loose!' He got the reaction he wanted. When he turned the lights back on, more than half the women were sitting, pale and rigid, with their feet up in the air."

Flossie, the tree-climber, also loved animals. "Flossie got the cutest little white dog. We were obsessed with that little dog, and wanted to stay home and play and play with it. We'd dress the dog up like a doll and take her for a ride in our doll buggies. That was much more fun than going to school." The imp in Lorene surfaced, as it often did. "How could I manage to stay home from school and play with the dog? Pink eye was spreading through the school. Flossie and I decided to tell our mothers that we had pink eye, very contagious. We put my sister Nina's rouge all over the outside of our eyes for a convincing effect, we thought." The mothers were not fooled.

Then there were the cats. There were two house cats, Fluffy and Caliban — and 26 more cats in the barn, with the family's two horses. "I brought home all the stray cats I could find," Lorene remarks. "My patient father had reached his limit. 'Now Lorene, if you bring another cat home, I'm going to kill the cat and spank you,' he told me firmly." She listened. "Spank me? Never in my life did my father spank me. He was so mild mannered. I knew he meant what he said!"

So there were no more stray cats brought home. Lorene could always find other channels for her seemingly limitless energy. She and Flossie would think up things to do, and this time, instead of climbing up, they tunneled down. "Flossie had two brothers and a sister. We dug tunnels." This was not casual tunnel digging; this was digging with a purpose. "We dug deep. We were going to use our tunnels to hide from the Germans, when they came to get us. We put boards over the entrance, to hide."

Fears were not foreign to a childhood then. The back drop of World War I had a marked impact, along with the encroaching Depression, transients and robberies, and the spread of tuberculosis. Erma Hildeman was a year older than Lorene, in eighth grade, when her mother died of tuberculosis. Her father had also died, so the Cuthbertsons took Erma in, "until the extended family could decide what to do with Erma and her two brothers." Erma stayed with Lorene's family for a full year, and joined Lorene in her love of music. "In school, we used to march in and out of the building to music. Erma and I played duets on two pianos so the kids could march back into school after recess." The two have stayed friends over more than seven decades. "We've always stayed in touch," Lorene states.

Another childhood memory from about age 12 centers on her "forced, somewhat of an emergency" driving lesson. "My father had to go away on business, catching the train at the edge of town. My mother didn't drive. So I rode to the train with my father driving the car, a Reo truck. Then I had to drive the car back home. I did a fine job until I didn't stop soon enough when positioning it in the barn, also used as our garage. I impaled the front of the truck, putting the fender right through the wood on the far side of the barn."

Sitting still and doing nothing was obviously not part of Lorene's "bag of tricks" as a young girl. Sundays were a day, however, when the family refrained from activity because of religious beliefs, a common practice then. So Lorene put her mind to work. "I'd heard that the manufacturer of Mentholatum, A.A. Hyde, was offering to give any child ten dollars who could learn the Sermon on the Mount, all three chapters. Since I couldn't do any physical things, like my tree climbing, on Sundays, I decided to give this a try. It was quite a thing. When through with the memory work, I had to recite the whole thing before the board of deacons of the church."

Lorene passed this memory test;

she'd learned the three chapters in their entirety. She knew immediately what she wanted to do with the hard-earned ten dollars. "Every day on my way to grade school, I had to pass by Carter's Jewelry Store. In the window was the most beautiful ruby ring. I couldn't keep my eyes from that, each day. So I went to Mr. Carter. 'How much is that ring?' I asked him. 'Fourteen dollars.' I didn't have it." But Lorene was not one to give in easily.

"I have ten dollars from reciting the Sermon on the Mount," she told him.

"I know," Mr. Carter replied. "Well, I get 25 cents allowance each week. Could I give you the ten dollars now, and then 25 cents each week, until the ring is paid for?" The ring was hers — for ten dollars.

"It is the most beautiful, large ruby solitaire," Lorene states. "I still have it." And she brings it out to be admired, still as pleased with it as she was those 80 years ago.

Typically, teenage years left some of the enchantment of younger years behind. Perhaps her family left something to be desired? Perhaps her parents weren't perfect? Maybe there was something better. At age 13 or 14, Marjorie, Florence and Lorene decided to find out.

"Our parents were not good to us, we were all sure. So we would run away." After some discussion, the teenaged trio decided on Washington, DC as their ideal destination, and the President and the First Lady as their new family. "We each wrote a letter to the First Lady."

"We would like to get out of a small town," we wrote. "We would like to work for the President of the United States."

Now came the real problem. How would they get letters back, inviting them to come, without their parents seeing the letters of invitation first and denying them the sure offer?

Again Lorene's quick mind and determination went to work. They would each receive mail under a pen name. "I chose 'Eleanor Walker' as my name," Lorene states. "My sister had a friend, Ethel McKean, who worked at the post office. We took her into our confidence, and she agreed to put aside any mail under our false names. Still, we rushed to the post office window every day, wanting to be sure we got there before anyone else in our families."

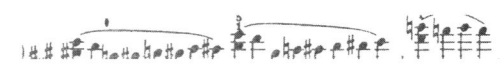

Each girl did receive a response from the White House — "not from the First Lady, but from some wise woman assistant. 'Stay in school and finish school,' the letters read. 'Then apply to us again.' I still think that was a remarkable thing to do for us. We took it to heart." Their excursion would wait, and school days in small-town Sterling would continue.

After Lorene started voice lessons at age 14, "I just kept on," she states simply. When she was a senior in high school, her music teacher sent her to the state music competition, where she took third place. Her interest in music, which has flourished for a lifetime, had budded early. There are not many vivid memories of music with her brother and sister. "Both were so much older than I." Church music always played a part, and she obviously had many friends to share her musical interests.

A cherished early memory, bearing a tangible witness to this day, is the camera her father gave her at her junior high school graduation. She was 12 years old. Eighty-two years later, at age 94, the camera is still with her, kept nearby in her room at the Anchorage Pioneers' Home where she lives today. It's a Folding Autographic Brownie, and she pats it as she remembers, "Everyone — lots of my school friends — wanted their picture taken with this. I still have some of their photos taken with this camera."

As clear as a photographic image are impressions from the summer following her junior year in high school. "There was a knock at our door that summer. It was our neighbor, Mr. Kilbourn, a rancher

Lorene with Eleanor Kilbourn, 1921, cooking for a month in the summer for ranch hands.

who owned a huge number of acres outside of town. He had five children — a son my age, a daughter two years younger than I, another daughter four years younger, and then twin girls. He had come to talk with my mother, telling her that his cook for the ranch harvesters, a widow named Mrs. Bertha Hall, was sick. The ranch hands were mostly college men from Sterling College. 'This has happened at a bad time,' he told my mother. 'The wheat is ripe, and I've got all these men I need someone to cook for. I know that your Lorene is a good cook. Could I borrow her? Could she come and cook for me along with my daughter Eleanor — until Bertha is back on her feet?'

"I was 16 at the time. I know my mother had some second thoughts — two young females surrounded by about a dozen college men? But she eventually agreed to let me go. I went out there and stayed right at the ranch with Eleanor who was 14. We had a bedroom downstairs, with all of the men staying in bedrooms upstairs. We all got along fine, as long as Eleanor and I could put up with the tricks they were always playing on us. The registers for the heat went directly from their rooms upstairs down to our room. Wouldn't it be fun, they thought — a real scream — to dangle a snake from their register down to ours? Well, they got the reaction they wanted from us. It was truly a scream!"

Instead of money, Lorene's payment for her efforts was a three-week trip to Colorado with the Kilbourns. "Mr. Kilbourn took the whole family and me, in two cars. I drove the Overland; he drove the Cadillac, all the way to Estes Park, camping along the way. It took us a week to get there. We had a grand time."

One thing learned from visiting with Lorene is that she "collects" people. People who have met her once resurface, weaving themselves back into her life, not wanting to lose touch, a testimonial to her ability to be "a part of all that she has met." Many years later, when Lorene was living in Alaska and went back to Steling for a visit, one of these "ranch hands" rediscovered her. "His name was Ted Warren. He came up to me one Sunday after church. 'I never did tell you,' he said to me. 'You know that corn bread you used to make for us at the ranch? Well, there were little weevils in it! I was afraid that if I told you then, you might leave in embarrassment, and then we'd have no cook.'"

High school years were packed with musical activities at school, in addition to her private piano and voice lessons. "I was in all the musical productions at the school," Lorene states. "Anything musical that came along, I was in! And I was on the debate team too."

Graduation came in the spring of 1922. That day, a quartet of friends spent the whole day together, before the evening ceremony. "Marjorie and I and our boyfriends rode out to my father's bottling works. Between the four of us, we drank a case of soda pop, 24 bottles of pop, before the ceremony. My father was such a generous man, he was glad to have us and to share with us. But how we managed to sit through the ceremony later that day, after all that soda, is beyond me!"

Unlike graduations today, made bitter sweet by the recognition that friends will most likely scatter geographically, Sterling High School graduates tended to stay there. "I knew I would stay in town right after high school," Lorene states simply. "Most of us went right on to studies at Sterling College. I always knew I would go there, and live at home. My parents were always glad to have my college friends come over to our home."

Lorene's closest college friend her first two years there was Mabel McKee, from Beloit, Kansas. "She sang in the glee club with me. Mabel's boyfriend was Ken Oliver and mine was Clifford Forney. Clifford and Ken were good friends, too, so the four of us often went riding in my boyfriend's big car — Clifford and I in front, and Mabel and Ken in back." Mabel and Ken would eventually marry and Lorene and Mabel's parents would become best friends.

Lorene at age 18 with Clifford Forney. "We're on the back steps of my home. Clifford was captain of the boys' basketball team and I was captain of the girls' team. We went together during our senior year in high school and for two years during college."

At the college, Lorene was a soprano soloist with the glee club. She was also the piano accompanist for the Sterling College orchestra. After freshman and sophomore years at Sterling College, the wanderlust struck Lorene. "By 1925, I wanted to see more than just Sterling," Lorene confesses. "I applied to a teachers' placement agency. Back then, you could teach after completing two years of college. Through the agency, I learned that Fromberg, Montana needed a music teacher for all grades combined with a seventh and eighth grade teaching position in geography and other subjects. I would receive $133 a month for this assignment. That was riches — double — compared to Sterling. Why, there a teacher made just $65 a month! So off I went. I felt I would be getting very rich, very fast."

Lorene taught school, all grades, in Fromberg, Montana in 1925 and '26, returning to Sterling in 1927, to finish her degree, a bachelor of science in music and home economics in the spring of 1928. It was while writing a term paper on Eskimos in Alaska at Sterling College that her interest in the far north territory was first peaked, prodding the beginnings of plans for a journey north. It was a journey that would eventually make a drastic difference to her new hometown, Anchorage, at the end of that road.

If her parents had wanted her to be "O.K." as a farmer cultivating fields, they would have been startled to see that down the road she chose she would become not just O.K., but "shining," a cultivator blazing new fields in the arts in Alaska, going farther west, a family tradition. The arts community in her new home would be forever enriched by her being there.

Lorene took the train from Denver to Billings, Montana to her first teaching assignment, Fromberg, Montana. "Here I'm with other teachers I met on the train. I've kept in touch with one of the teachers, Lois Heginbotham, for over 70 years. In 1926, I sang at her wedding in Colorado."

Lorene, about 1910, with her Grandma and Grandpa Dunlap who lived with Lorene's family. On the right is Lorene's cousin, Harold Dunlap. "He was from Girard, Kansas, and the only cousin near my own age."

Kanza Camp Fire Group, after a council meeting, at their Guardian or leader's home, Florence Grizzell — June 1921.

After a Camp Fire meeting, the Kanza Camp Fire girls — "We were a close knit group!"

Mostly Music

Camp Fire girls grow older still, but ties remain strong. (Lorene is in the middle row, second from the right.)

Mabel McKee Oliver with her husband, Ken, after 62 years of marriage.

Kanza Camp Fire reunion — "We meet again, all grown up and married." Left to right: Mary, Nina, Alberta, Florence, Lorene (in the middle), Claire, Wilma, Florence.

Chapter Two
The Early Teaching Years

"Lorene had a merry heart — and how could we help but sing!"
(Marie Fahrenbruch, one of Lorene's first high school students)

All through her life, Lorene has been a teacher, sometimes hired formally as a school teacher, and at other times taking young people "under her wing" more informally, to assist them in many ways.

Her first official teaching assignment was the one in Fromberg, Montana. Lorene calls Fromberg "a small little place, a sugar beet community of perhaps 1,000 people." In 1925, there were two separate buildings for the school, one for kindergarten through grade eight and a second building for high school classes. Lorene taught in both buildings. "Lots of the students came into school on horse back or horse and buggy. When I arrived there to teach music in all grades and some junior high subjects, the students had never had music in school. They clamored for music. I was just 19 years old and those high school kids related to me so well that 'little Fromberg' won the Eastern Montana Music Meet! The town went crazy with excitement." Lorene remembers calling her parents back in Kansas, to tell them of the victory.

One of those students kept in touch with Lorene over the many decades since those first teaching days in Fromberg. Lorene fosters friendships and tends to them, and her friend collection is diminished only by the fact that she has outlived so many of them.

Marie Fahrenbruch is that student who kept in touch for so long. Her married name was Marie Prichard, and she recently died. Marie was a senior in the school glee club that "Miss Cuthbertson" had started. Lorene calls her and her younger brother Fred "some of my favorite people." Their parents were immigrants from Germany and hardly spoke any English. "I think we all became so close because they really depended on me," Lorene states. The family was poor, and their German heritage against a background of World War I did not help the family make friends.

A letter written by Marie in 1954 attests to the bonds Miss Lorene Cuthbertson formed with her students and the lasting influence her caring had on students' lives. (Marie wrote the letter in support of Lorene's candidacy for Alaska's Golden Rule Mother that year.)

"Lorene certainly had a merry heart — and how could we help but sing! ... The year that Lorene directed our glee club, we responded so well to her personality that we were privileged to travel about the state in contest with large cities, and when we ended up — we were first place in the Eastern Montana Music Meet and second in the entire state. If you were acquainted with

Fromberg High School girls' gee club – The small Montana town had never had music in the school when Lorene arrived in 1925, at age 19. She organized a high school glee club and took the girls' glee club on to win state music competitions.

little Fromberg, you would understand why this seemed such a record for us!"

Marie goes on to give Lorene credit for much more than just musical mentoring. "Besides the glee club, Lorene was the center of all the worthwhile activities in our little town — plays, sports, church programs, school programs — and she could plan, direct, and inspire us all without any apparent effort. My mental picture of Lorene right now is of her sitting at the piano, directing, singing with a great smile, with that overflowing merry heart! She is still that way, isn't she?"

Many people, inspired by Lorene and her merry heart over the years, would answer, "Yes."

Lorene had planned to teach one year in Fromberg and then return to Sterling College to continue her education. "But a nice salary increase induced me to stay another year." That, and the fact that she was very happy there. She lived in a rooming house "on a pretty knoll" with three other women teachers, each paying $40 a month for room and board. The house was owned by Mrs. Lester,

Lorene with a Fromberg teacher roommate and the roommate's boy friend — "Even way back I was wearing hats!"

and she placed the teachers in two rooms, two to a bed. Lorene remembers her as a wonderful cook, milking her cow, churning her butter, and placing it in a wonder — a Kelvinator refrigerator. "It was the first refrigerator many of us had ever seen — electric!"

In addition to her refrigerator, Mrs. Lester was also the proud owner of a baby grand piano. Why? Lorene was never sure, since her landlady never played it, but Lorene took full advantage of this luxury and played it "all the time."

Weekends were often spent hiking in the surrounding countryside and into the foothills. She'd have on her knickers, the only time she would think of wearing pants.

One of her frequent hiking companions was George O'Connor, a senior at the high school and another Fromberg student with whom Lorene kept in contact until his death a few years ago. "The whole O'Connor family adopted me," Lorene states. "George was the oldest of four children – two boys and two girls. His father had one of two grocery stores in town,

Lorene with George O'Connor, whom she met in Fromberg, MT— "He's the one I almost married. This picture was obviously taken many years later here in Anchorage at my daughter, Carol Anne's home. We're both in our 80s in the photo. Behind us is a quilt that had been my mother's. She traveled with it in a covered wagon from Ohio to Kansas when she was just two years old."

and George worked there after school. His interests were more intellectual than musical, but we drew very close."

Their friendship bond could have become a marriage bond, when George proposed to Lorene some six decades after their Fromberg years, when both were in their 80s. "By then, health problems intervened, and we obviously never did marry." Asked if she wishes events had turned out otherwise and she and George had married, Lorene responds with her usual acceptance of a life taken on its own terms. "No, I've been very happy following the course my life has taken since." Eventually eight proposals of marriage would come Lorene's way.

In addition to her teaching responsibilities in Fromberg, Lorene was directing a church choir and coaching the girls' basketball team her second year in Fromberg. The team went on to win the county championship and once again "the town went wild."

The summers of 1926 and 1928 will always be special to Lorene. It was during those two summers that she worked and entertained at Yellowstone National Park.

Lorene (back row, second from left) as girls' basketball coach her second year of teaching in Fromberg, MT — She led the team to victory, just as she had the girls' glee club!

Chapter Three
Yellowstone Summers
"Hasher" or "Pillow Puncher"?

*I*t was while Lorene was teaching that first year in Fromberg that she got a wire from a family friend. Reverend Hutchinson, an outreach minister from Pittsburgh, Pennsylvania, had stayed with Lorene's family in Sterling, Kansas when he would travel west for summer conferences at the Sterling Presbyterian Church. Lorene had gotten to know him as one of many guests in her childhood home. "Rev. Hutchinson had heard that I was teaching in Montana, and he had a trip scheduled to Billings. He wanted to know if I could meet him so we could visit."

In the course of their conversations, Rev. Hutchinson began speaking about his travels to Yellowstone National Park and Lady Mac, the manager of the camp there. The talk ignited Lorene's desire for adventure. "Oh, it would be fun to work there," Lorene remembers telling him, after he explained that summer employees were college students or recent college graduates from all over the country. "I'll write to Lady Mac," he told her.

Lorene was told she could work at Yellowstone's Canyon Camp, either as a "hasher" (waitress) or "pillow puncher" (a "tent girl" taking care of the cabins). She would provide her own transportation to the park and would receive $15 a month for her work there.

Lorene chose pillow puncher. She traveled to Yellowstone with one of her best friends from Sterling, Mabel McKee, who would work there too, but as a hasher. They joined the other 150 summer employees working in one of four camps in the park.

Mostly Music

Lorene joins her fellow "hashers" and "pillow punchers" – "all college students from all over the country" – the summer of 1926, all employees at Canyon Camp, Yellowstone National Park. (She's 9th from the left in the 5th row!)

Yellowstone Park's Canyon Camp – "We'd sit on logs around a campfire. There was a different musical program there in the outdoor amphitheater every night of the week."

Soon soprano strains of *The Indian Love Call* could be heard coming from the woods in the evenings. That was Lorene, combining her soprano voice with that of a baritone in a popular duet. Not surprisingly, she had not restricted her talents to daytime pillow punching, but had branched out to evening entertaining.

"There was a large outdoor amphitheater," Lorene recalls, "with huge logs for people to sit on. We put on a different musical program every night of the week. I'd play the piano, and there would also be community singing, which I often conducted."

After the evening program, Lorene would join a group of her newfound friends and they'd all go out together. Here, as wherever she would go, she collected friends. She returned to the park for a second summer there in 1928. A little book called Haynes Guide to Yellowstone National Park, first published in 1912 and kept by Lorene as a remembrance of her Yellowstone summers, is full of notes, penned by those friends 70 years ago. Many are testimonials to Lorene's good humor, talents and friendliness. Some suggest what lay ahead for Lorene, a grand adventure to come.

One of these, which still brings a smile to Lorene, is written in poetry form.

The Eskimo sleeps in his white bear skin
And is kept very warm, I am told.
Last night I slept in my white bare skin
And caught a hell of a cold.

Lorene "collected friends" in Yellowstone, a lifelong hobby of hers. "This is Bob Polk, my 'best boyfriend' the summer of '26."

Another penned in faded ink, reads, "Good luck in Alaska," from "Woody."

It was toward the end of 1928, Lorene's second summer at Yellowstone National Park, that she learned she would be traveling to Anchorage, Alaska to become the town's first public school music teacher.

Chapter Four
North to Alaska

"You have been elected to teach music and home economics. Wire your immediate acceptance." — Telegram from Cecil Sly, superintendent of Anchorage schools — 1928.

The clipping from an August, 1928 edition of a newspaper, the Sterling, Kansas *Bulletin,* reads, "Miss Lorene Cuthbertson, who is now in Yellowstone Park, received word last Monday that she had been elected to a position as teacher of home economics and music at the high school in Anchorage, Alaska. She has wired her acceptance, and in company with Miss Lois Lehman of Halstead, niece of Mrs. J.T. Tyrell, of this city, who will teach in the same place, will sail on the steamer Yukon from Seattle, Washington, on August 18. They will leave the boat at Seward, and go by rail over 100 miles to their destination of Anchorage. They expect to arrive there about August 27."

That estimated arrival date proved accurate. Lorene and Lois did arrive in Anchorage on August 27, 1928.

After her first summer at Yellowstone, Lorene had returned to Kansas to complete her degree at Sterling College. Her teaching assignment in Fromberg, Montana had been carried out before receiving her degree. Lorene comments, "In those years, one could teach after two years of college, with a special certificate. It was common practice."

She received her degree from Sterling College on May 31, 1928, a Bachelor of Arts degree in home economics.

It was while finishing up her course work during her senior year, in a home economics course on the family, that she had been given the assignment to write a term paper about a different ethnic group. She chose the Alaska Eskimo as her topic. Very little information on Alaska was available in the library, but Lorene remembers getting out a book of maps and finding the names of Alaska's larger towns written in big letters –- Ketchikan, Anchorage, Juneau, Fairbanks. She found herself picking up her pen and writing letters addressed simply to "the superintendent of schools" in each one of those bigger Alaska cities, "to see if they could send me any information for my research paper."

Back came a letter from the superintendent of schools in Ketchikan, Mr. Burdick. He had gone to school in Kansas and shared mutual acquaintances with Lorene and her family. (One is often tempted to declare that there are no strangers in Lorene's life. She has seemingly woven a far-reaching pattern of people connections around herself, one that she has always tended with care.) "In his letter, Mr. Burdick suggested that I apply for teaching jobs in Alaska. 'I think you'd like it here,' he wrote although there were no openings at the time in Ketchikan. However, he sent me the names of the superintendents in the other three towns," Lorene remembers.

She was immediately intrigued. She has always had what she calls "a little horizon interest. I yearned for adventure, and knew I wanted to see more than just Sterling, Kansas." She'd already accepted a position for the fall in Americus, Kansas as a music teacher. "I wasn't very excited about it, really. I had really liked Montana, Yellowstone and the West." She sent off the letters to the other superintendents, with her teaching qualifications.

Letters from the superintendents in both Juneau and Fairbanks came back to her, and in each case there were no vacancies.

At the end of July, 1928, a telegram came to Lorene in Canyon Camp, Yellowstone National Park, where she was working for her second summer, after her college graduation. The telegram was from Cecil Sly, the superintendent of schools in Anchorage, and its few words would prove to be some of the most pivotal in Lorene's life.

"You have been elected to teach

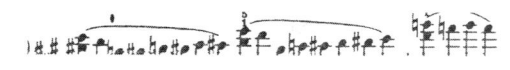

music and home economics. Wire your immediate acceptance," it read.

Full of excitement, of course she did just that — then faced the matter of informing her parents. She sent them a telegram with her news. "This almost put my mother to bed," Lorene states. "Who knew anything about Alaska in 1928? My mother knew more about India or Africa. There were missionaries there. But Alaska ? No. She pictured me going by train to Seattle, Washington, then by ship ten days north — she was sure she'd never see her 'baby' again!"

There would be no time to return to Sterling and pack her things. Superintendent Sly had informed her that she would need to be in Anchorage by August 27. She had three weeks to get there. She was also told that her salary would be $180 a month. "That seemed sky high to me then," she says. "My friends teaching in Kansas were getting $60 a month. Imagine — I'd be getting three times that amount. I was sure I'd be rich."

There was no doubt in Lorene's mind that she would be going north to Alaska. She made her travel plans. She'd take the train from Yellowstone to Seattle, a trip of a night and a day. Her ticket for the week-and-a-half steamer journey from Seattle to Seward, Alaska would cost $60. Then she'd need a train ticket from Seward to Anchorage, since there was no link by roadway. "I had just one month to get everything ready."

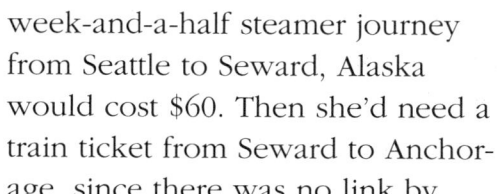

Her enthusiasm was in marked contrast to her parents' reluctance, worried to see their daughter going so far to what they likened to a vast unknown. "My daughter is going to Alaska!" her mother told family friends and acquaintances, her concern readily apparent. When she heard of another young woman from Kansas, heading to Alaska to teach at the same time, her mother grasped on to the news. Her daughter could have a traveling companion. That would lessen her anxiety.

Lois Lehman lived in Halstead, Kansas. She was a little older than Lorene, and would be teaching second grade in Anchorage. Mrs. Cuthbertson hopped on a train to Halstead to meet Lois. It was quickly decided that Lois and Lorene would meet up in Seattle and journey on to Anchorage together. "This travel plan eased my mother's mind a bit." Meanwhile Lorene had her mother send her clothing, especially her warmer things, to Seattle.

Lorene and Lois met in a hotel in Seattle, on the eve of their steamer trip north. "We got along like two peas in a pod," according to Lorene. With Lois was another young woman, Vera Lynn Jones, from Great Bend, Kansas. "Vera was on her way to Alaska 'for better or worse,'" Lorene states. "She was to meet her fiance at our boat terminus, Seward. He would marry her there and take her 30 miles beyond Anchorage to live, to what was then called simply 'Matanuska.'"

The trip on the steamer, Yukon, proved to be a story in itself. "The boat stopped at every little place, night and day," Lorene remembers. Soon after boarding on August 18, she bumped into a friend of her sister's, Ben Ficken, who had gone to college with Nina. He was traveling with his brother and a male friend, so there was immediately a core group of young people sharing the adventure, sailing north. "You can well imagine that we six Kansans — reared within a radius of 100 miles — enjoyed our trip as far as Juneau together."

Much of the trip is recorded in Lorene's own words, printed in an article in the Sterling, Kansas *Bulletin*, dated April 25, 1929. Lorene begins, "Dear Sterling friends: Several requests have come for me to write a letter telling of my trip to and experiences in Alaska." After relating how the Kansas group of six found each other, she tells of sailing north.

To Ketchikan

"Leaving Seattle, we steamed out of Elliott Bay through the waters of Puget Sound. We crossed the boundary line separating the State of Washington from British Columbia about 4 p.m. Saturday. Out of Seattle, our first stop was Ketchikan, which was reached on Monday. Here, we visited a large salmon cannery that was just closing its season. The curio shops were also very interesting. Ketchikan is a typical Alaskan town built at the foot of the mountains.

To Wrangell
"Delayed by fog, we were anchored for ten hours waiting for high tide before entering Wrangell Narrows. Wrangell, on Wrangell Island, was reached through the tortuous rock-strewn Wrangell Narrows. Wrangell might be called the town of totem poles. Here lives Pat Cotter, the author of an Alaska history, and we were lucky to see and talk with him.

To Juneau
"We arrived in Juneau about midnight on Wednesday. It is curious to

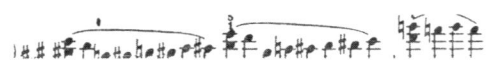

note that all curio shops open for the incoming of steamers no matter what the hour of arrival may be. We were in Juneau several hours and noticed many signs of welcome for Sec. Jardine who visited Alaska this summer. The largest gold quartz mill is located here, as is also the Alaska museum. The capital city is very beautifully situated at the foot of Mt. Juneau and in all respects seems to be a thriving little city. Here at Juneau the men in our party left to continue their journey to Baranoff Island on a small mail boat. (They were going hunting.) We hated to see them go, but all good things must come to an end."

While the Yukon was docked in Juneau, Lorene noticed a young woman about her own age, getting on board the boat. Lorene was drawn to her, since she spotted the violin case the woman was carrying. Lorene learned her name was Rica Niemi. She was born in Finland, had been living in Douglas, just outside of Juneau, and had been working at the Palace Theater in Juneau as a violinist, part of an orchestra that accompanied the movies. There was no bridge linking the two towns at that time, so Rica was a frequent traveler on the connecting ferry.

Rica was voyaging to Anchorage and then on to Wasilla where she, too, would teach school. She would be living in an area then known as Swamp View, 3.9 miles outside of Wasilla proper along the railroad, and her living quarters would be attached to the one-room school. She had been told that her class load would consist of eight students spread over grades one to twelve. Lorene remembers, "Rica was pleased to find two other young women, sailing north to teach, myself and Lois, along with Vera heading north to her groom." (Rica is now Rica Swanson, age 94. Lorene and Rica have maintained their friendship over the seven intervening decades. Today Rica lives in the Anchorage Pioneers' Home with her husband, Frank Swanson, in the same building with Lorene.)

The Yukon departed Juneau, with something other than smooth sailing ahead. Lorene continues her printed travelogue. "And now the only unpleasant part of our week's journey. Upon sailing out on the Gulf of Alaska, most of the people gave the fish a chance to say 'Thanks' for a good dinner. However, I am so Scotch that I would not be caught doing a thing like that. Across the Gulf of Alaska we reached Cordova, the 'Copper Gateway.' This part of the trip affords the thrill of a real ocean voyage. Cordova also is an up-and-coming little city and the point of ingress to Interior Alaska by way of the Copper River Railway and the Richardson Highway.

To Valdez and Columbia Glacier
"Valdez, our next stopping place, is the coast terminus of the Richardson Highway, which, with the Yukon Highway, forms an unbroken stretch of automobile road 536 miles in length, stretching from Valdez to Circle on the Yukon River. Here at Valdez, U.S. Marshall Sullivan invited us to pick flowers –- the typical Alaska pansies that put pansies in the States to shame, both for size and coloring. The California poppies certainly could not bloom fairer in their native state than they bloom here. We were also given the golden opportunity of picking luscious big strawberries from Mr. Sullivan's patch.

"Our next stop was at Columbia Glacier, one of the most enjoyable and impressive sights of our entire trip. This indeed we shall never forget. Huge pieces of ice continually breaking and crashing into the sea with a mighty roar, was a thrill entirely new and foreign to us. From here we went on to Latouche, nothing more than a cannery center, and headquarters for 'herring chokers.'

To Seward
"Saturday morning we steamed into Resurrection Bay at the head of which is Seward. Here Miss Jones' fiancé met us, and in an hour the wedding ceremony was over. It doesn't take long in Alaska!" Lorene explains that she and Lois were witnesses at the Seward wedding, although they'd known the bride, Vera, for only a week and the groom for just minutes. Lorene describes Seward of 1928 as "mostly just a terminus for boats and the lower end of the railroad, not really a developed town." Bride and groom stayed a few days to see the beauty of the mountains around Seward, "and the others of us started on our 'final lap.'"

On to Anchorage
That final lap, from Seward to Anchorage, was by rail. Lorene remembers that the train ride "set the stage" for what has since been her unending love of Alaska. Her introduction to Alaska, as the train looped along, left her in awe. "The ride of 114 miles we found to be the most beautiful of the entire trip, and in spite of being very tired, we enjoyed it immensely….There were innumer-

able beautiful little mountain streams coming down the sides of the green mountains by which we were continuously surrounded. Lakes abound along the tracks. Most of them were quite large, glassy, and had a bath house and beach. You can picture for yourself the reflection of the mountains in the water. Lovely!

"Twenty–three miles out from Seward, we stopped at Nellie Neil's (Lawing's) place. She is one of Alaska's 'relics.' In her day she was a great huntress and had many of the animals which she killed stuffed and mounted. She was married not too many years ago to some old 'sourdough'… and the ceremony was performed in the theatre in Seward, with 25 cents admittance. How's that for making money?"

When sharing this particular memory seven decades later, Lorene added some details. Nellie's cabin had been on Kenai Lake, and she had originally been from Colorado. In order to visit Nellie's cabin and its collection of mounted animals, admission was free – but it cost each visitor 25 cents to get out. Her printed newspaper article continues. "At about 12:30 noon we got to the famous 'loop' in the railroad where you can see three spirals where you have been or will be. It's in a beautiful location. At the very bottom of the loop there is a little sandwich shop where we bought a sandwich and cup of coffee for 25 cents. Rather we felt the irresistible urge for more food, so parted with half a dollar.

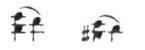

"Along the mountain side, our attention was called to a bunch of mountain goats, the prize game for every hunter. When we got within about 25 miles from Anchorage, we spied Cook's Inlet, the edge of which we followed the rest of the way. Cook's Inlet has the second highest tide in the world, the Bay of Fundy having first. Here, at high tide, the water rises 36 feet. You can imagine the miles and miles of sand beach we have at low water. The tide changes every six hours, and all plans for boating have to be made accordingly. The railroad runs in a most advantageous place – the mountains towering up on one side, and the Inlet beach on the other. We arrived at Anchorage station, our destination, about 3:30 p.m."

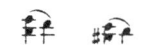

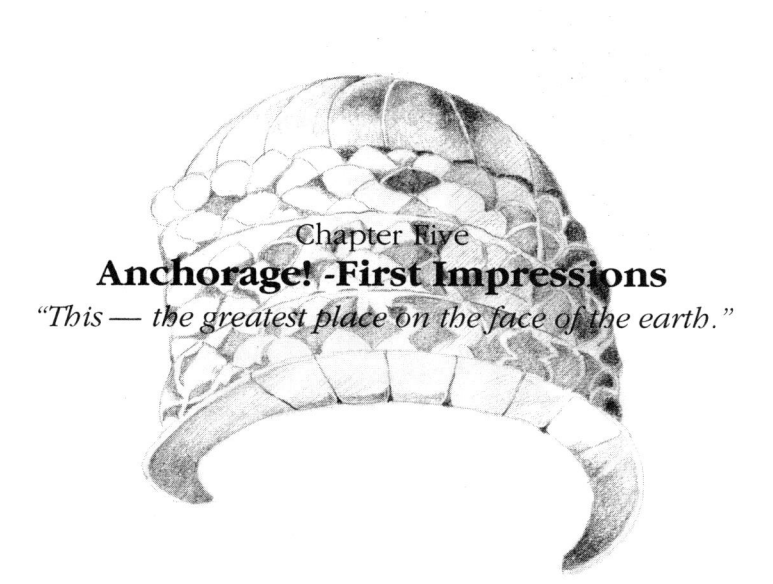

Chapter Five
Anchorage! - First Impressions
"This — the greatest place on the face of the earth."

There she was, Miss Lorene Cuthbertson, age 23, in what would be her new home, and where she was to find herself the first public school music teacher the community of Anchorage, in the Territory of Alaska, had ever known.

It is not overstating to declare that it was "love at first sight," certainly on Lorene's part, and almost certainly on the part of her new hometown. "I was thrilled to be in Anchorage," Lorene states, her enthusiasm only made stronger by the more than 70 intervening years. "I was surely guided by a kind and wise Creator to this, the greatest place on the face of the earth, in my evaluation. My life has been full of activity, creativity, love, and fulfillment. What more could one desire?" To chronicle what has taken place in Anchorage, since Lorene took those first steps off the train in 1928, is a monumental task. Trace the trails of so many music, civic and arts organizations in today's Anchorage, and they lead back to Anne Lorene Cuthbertson's first footsteps off the train and into town.

Even those first footsteps did not go unnoticed. Lorene comments, "At this time in Anchorage history, train arrivals were an important occasion." Three new teachers coming into town – Lorene, Lois and Rica — would be cause for considerable attention. "When the young school teachers arrived in such an isolated place as Anchorage was in those days, why everybody was down at the train and by the time you got off, they knew the color of your eyes, how old you were, and how much you weighed! It was really quite fun! And the school board members were very careful with us from the beginning — watching over us."

Lorene remembers being met by a bus at the train station and taken to the Anchorage Hotel.

Lorene's first impressions come back to us, fresh and accurate, since they, too, were recorded in the Sterling, Kansas *Bulletin* in her article dated April 25, 1929, eight months after she arrived.

She wrote, "We have found Anchorage by far the best planned and laid-out town that we saw since leaving the States. It is built on a large plateau with Cook's Inlet on the north and west, and the mountains averaging about 12 miles away on the east and south. There are many lovely hikes one can take in these mountains. It is the Chugach Range.

"At one time Anchorage was a thriving town of about 10,000 due to gold and coal mines in the mountains and to the five canneries. At present, the population is nearly 3,000." (Today, she states that it was 2,500.) "We were almost disappointed because everything is so modern. We (Lorene and Lois) were taken from the station in a big Gray Line bus the same as you find in any city, to the Anchorage Hotel where we had a nice large room and bath connected. In the parlor is a mammoth picture of Mt. McKinley by the Alaskan artist, Sydney Laurence. The hotel management has a standing offer of $10,000 for it. The Parsons Hotel is very nice too. There are several teachers staying at each of these hotels for the winter. The Empress Theater is very nice. It has quite a large pipe organ, and the present

"Anchorage, as it looked when I arrived! This photo is dated 1930. I knew I was in the greatest place on the face of the earth."

organist has just come from playing with the Pantages Circuit on the Pacific coast.

"We have the best hospital in Western Alaska here, a dental clinic, a large number of good cafes, modern refrigerated meat markets, seven taxi concerns, dandy groceries, a Rexall Drug Store besides several privately owned ones, fur shops, three photograph galleries, novelty shops, jewelry stores, magazine stands, and in fact, I can think of nothing we lack." One can imagine Lorene sighing with relief as she wrote, "We even get the popular records and sheet music from Seattle."

Exploring her new home verbally, Lorene continued in the article, "One of the salmon canneries alone which does a very thriving business in the summer time shipped 32,000 cases this year. They hire around 200 people. Anchorage is the headquarters for the Alaska Railroad, operated by the Department of the Interior, and the offices and machine shops are here. We have a daily newspaper relaying the scandals from the States. There is one of the three radio broadcasting stations in Alaska located here – KFQD. The Elks lodge has a fine large building and the Odd Fellows and Shriners both have nice halls. They are all quite active. Every winter there are one or two home-talent plays besides the high school plays and operettas. People up here have lots of pep and apparently all the money they can spend. Most everybody has a car, and there are only a few miles – in fact, just 26 – of road from the town. The towns are so far apart that you have to go by train. Fully half of the town's population live in apartments. The residence section really isn't anything to write home about. The sidewalks are cement; we have electric street lights; the best fire department you ever saw for this size place; an airplane which carries furs, mail and passengers; the Alaska Road Commission offices are here; a baseball diamond with stadium; two tennis courts, ad infinitum."

So much energy, raw material, new ground to cultivate, people more than willing to have Lorene Cuthbertson lead them culturally into new territory. She was ready and eager to help, to polish up her new town. When, at age 94, Lorene Cuthbertson Harrison was asked recently, "Why have you done so much?", she replied simply, "Because there was so much that needed to be done – so much that needed someone to do it."

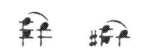

Chapter Six
More First Impressions
Lorene's First Months in Anchorage

Lorene wrote a second installment of her first impressions of Alaska and Anchorage, published in the Sterling, Kansas *Bulletin* the week after her first article. On May 2, 1929, her written record of her first months continues. "The idea prevalent that Alaska is a land of ice and snow is certainly false! We had our first snowfall October 18 and snow has continued off and on with our last bit March 22. Only one day did it in any way resemble the old Kansas blizzards....Of course the snow stays on the ground from the first snow till the last. Consequently, we saw many wagons converted into sleighs, but we have only two dog teams here. Only three days during the winter did the thermometer drop as low as 17 degrees below zero."

Contrasting the darkness of her first winter with the brightness of spring, Lorene continued, "During December and January the electric lights were only turned off during the noon hour, while now we wake up in the morning at 5:30 with the sun shining and it is light outside till 8 at night."

She picked up quickly on some of the local terminology. "The people here have some very queer expressions. For instance, when someone goes to the States, they go 'out.' 'Were you out this summer?' or 'Are you going to be in all winter?' are very common sentences here. Several years ago when people were here they were really 'in solitude,' away from the world entirely, and the expressions originated then. Also, until a person has been in Alaska long enough to see the Yukon freeze then thaw - in other words, practically a year - he is called a 'cheechako.' After the year has passed he is termed a 'sourdough.' Some of the sourdoughs are real 'characters,' certainly."

Lorene then changed the scope of her commentary, describing what she saw beyond Anchorage. "Mt. McKinley is only a distance of 154 miles from Anchorage. On a clear day it is very visible across the Inlet. It has been scaled by only two men – the Superintendent of McKinley National Park – Mr. Harry P. Karstens, and Archdeacon Stuck. It is 20, 800 feet high – the highest in North America. The U. S. Government operates a National Park and game reserve there which is visited by tourists annually.

"Just 23 miles north of Anchorage is the Matanuska Valley, the garden spot of Alaska. There is an experimental farm there sponsored by the Government. Mr. Snodgrass, from Kansas State Agricultural College, is the head of it, and his family is here each winter for the school term. I have seen some of the vegetables which were raised there, and I have never seen any in the States to compare with them. At the fair here there were cabbages so large that a wash tub wouldn't fit over them. Mr. Snodgrass says Kansas never grew such wheat as comes from here, either. There is a dairy project in connection with it which seems to be working out fine. We hope there will soon be some keen competition as far as milk is concerned for we pay 25 cents a quart for fresh milk. Canned milk is used almost entirely.

"Fox farming is quite an important industry. There are a dozen or so fox farms just close to Anchorage. All kinds of trapping is done. A large number of the high school boys go out every weekend into the mountains to their trap lines. Usually two or three go together on it, have a cabin near their line, and stay there Friday and Saturday nights.

"Prices in general really aren't as high as we expected. Milk and meat are the highest. A pork roast for three of us costs a dollar, canned goods are all a little higher, as everything is sold by even charge. There are no $3.98 sales here – it would be $3.95 or $4.00. The P.O. and banks are the only places that will take pennies. Canned salmon costs a little more here than in the States, owing to the fact that it is shipped to Seattle for labels, and the shipping cost both ways must be added.

"We get our mail only once a week – with the exception of every third week, when an extra boat brings mail into Seward on Saturday and the train brings it here on Monday. That's a great day!

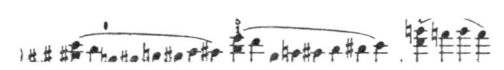

"Yet somehow we don't miss it coming every day as we had at first dreaded. We have a Government telegraph station here so in case of necessity, word could be received, or sent quickly."

Though certainly not a large town when Lorene and the other new school teachers arrived, they quickly found much to do within it. "It seems as though we are swamped with parties and dinner invitations. We seldom have more than a night or two a week alone. I believe the most fun we have had was at our 'upside down, backwards' bridge party. There are Catholic, Christian Science, Lutheran, and Presbyterian churches here. I think membership of the Presbyterian church is probably the largest.

"In the winter time the popular sports are skiing, tobogganing, and ice skating. Owing to the lack of enough cold weather this year, there was not one bit of skating. There was a huge toboggan slide down the hillside only a few blocks from school.

"I think nearly two-thirds of the men in town went across the bay or into the mountains hunting this fall. We were invited to several duck dinners, and had moose steak and mountain sheep steak given to us. The sheep meat is delicious! No, the moose wasn't so bad, either.

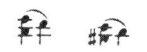

"Right now the excitement about the ice pool is running high. It costs $1 to take a chance of winning around $50,000. You must guess the exact date, hour and minute that the thaw comes and the ice pool of the Tanana River breaks....

"As far as climate, good times, and fine people are concerned, there's no doubt but that I am in the right town. In every respect it is as modern here as in Sterling. I live in a three-room steam-heated apartment by myself, in spite of the fact that I seldom find myself alone....I certainly shall never regret for a minute my year spent here. I plan staying until August sometime, when several of the high school folks will go 'out' with me (to college)....Au revoir till August – Lorene Cuthbertson."

Lorene returned to Kansas the summer of 1929. She had taken a teaching job in Pawnee Rock, Kansas, in order to be nearer to her parents in Sterling. It is easy to sense that it was something she felt she should do, but that she would be leaving with a reluctant heart. She left not knowing if she would see Alaska again – not knowing how many more Alaska summers she would eventually be seeing.

Chapter Seven
First Notes - Let the Music Begin!

*L*orene has a mind for memories. Beyond what is contained in these printed newspaper columns, she can bring back other vivid memories of the first year of teaching in Anchorage. The Alaska Fair that August was held downtown on Fourth Avenue, "the main drag," as she calls it. That was when Lorene first spotted those enormous vegetables mentioned in her newspaper columns sent back to Sterling. "Horses and wagons were pulled up at the end of the street. Farmers were displaying and selling pumpkins, lettuce, zucchini, cucumbers – such big ones!"

As is the case with the Alaska State Fair today, north in the valley town of Palmer, entertainment was a part of the early fair festivities. One can imagine the eyes of the young school teacher lighting up as she made contact with whatever cultural and entertainment groups were in her new, young city. Typically, she jumped right in — with both feet — and in a matter of days from stepping off the train.

"Maurice Sharp was in charge of the program entertainment for the fair. He had been involved in musical comedy back in Chicago, and was in Anchorage working as a chemist for the railroad. Also involved in community culture was Billy Murray, who owned a laundry. Billy would eventually marry Marion Ollerinshaw, who was coming to town with us on the Yukon, to be the organist at the Empress Theater." Billy and Maurice got in touch with

Mostly Music

the new music teacher in town, "and within days I was performing!" Back came the "Indian Love Call" of Lorene's Yellowstone days, with Marion accompanying her at the Empress on the organ. "I believe that the 'Indian Love Call' was the first song I sang in Anchorage," Lorene says. Who could have known how far those first notes, her first involvement in singing in Alaska, would reverberate through the musical

singing 'You're the Cream in My Coffee.' There was also a radio program called 'The Arctic Ice Worms,' a short program in the evenings. Soon I was invited to join in that program. Nell Hewitt played the piano for the radio station. She also played for all the funerals, until I was in town and could also play for some of them.

"There was also a little theater

Anchorage Public School on Fifth Avenue (where the Performing Arts Center is today) - This is where Lorene taught in 1928-1929.

history of the Anchorage-to-come?

Other seeds of culture were heard over the one radio station, KFQD. "Bill Wagner owned the station. I can still remember the first thing I heard over the radio – Vanny Jones

group, headed by Gus Gellis, who performed a lot of the important parts in the plays, and Bert Wennerstrom. Their productions were held in the Elks Hall."

Lorene remembers there were no

formal glee clubs or choirs, and there seemed to be far more men than women here. "The ten-men-to-every-women we sometimes hear about as legend did appear to exist then," Lorene states. It was as if she had discovered much raw creative energy and potential, just waiting to be harnessed and organized. "The people who were living here were innovative – or they wouldn't be living here. Within myself I knew that I was here to perform this mission, and it didn't take long for me to realize that it was happening!"

As the first public school music teacher the town had ever known, she quite naturally turned some of her focus to the school children, and found a ready audience for her desire to bring music and singing north. "The school was on Fifth Avenue. Anchorage Public School had six high school teachers in 1928, and a teacher for each lower grade – 15 teachers in all. After school, I would play the popular sheet music on the school piano, and the kids would gather around and sing with me. Some of them wanted to hear me play classical things. I decided that they would be my first focus; I would see what I could do with the high school kids. And were they ever receptive – raring to go!

"So right away, in September, I organized a high school choral group. By December, we were ready for our first production, Anchorage's first operetta, *Miss Cherry Blossom*." On Friday evening, December 14, 1928, the Japanese operetta in three acts was presented in full costume at the Empress Theatre. To this day, it retains its glow and status as one of her favorite projects.

New cultural ground had been broken. The following day, The *Anchorage Daily Times* proclaimed its success in the paper's headlines. "Student Players Delight Audience in Musical Show," the main headline read, followed by the subheading, "Miss Cherry Blossom Scored Big Hit at Empress Last Evening." The review begins, "The Anchorage public is indebted to the students of the high school for an evening of rare enjoyment, the operetta, *Miss Cherry Blossom*, which was presented at the Empress Theatre last night under the direction of Miss Lorene Cuthbertson, having proved one of the most pleasing entertainments ever staged in Anchorage." The lengthy article, full of praise for the specially designed oriental settings, the dancing, and splendid costuming, also contains acclamations for Superintendent Cecil Sly for his direction of the orchestra, and Mrs. Billy Murray for her organ and piano playing. There is also a long listing of the names of students in the two choruses, the Geisha girls and the American chorus. Some of the names from those youthful choruses would be very recognizable to the Anchorage community today.

addition to her music and home economics classes. She recalls, laughing heartily, how this assignment kept her on her toes. "I had never taken general science, but you know in a small school you have to teach things

Lorene's 8th grade sewing class at Anchorage Public School. First row, left to right: Aileen (last name unknown), Elsie Peterson, Bertha Crawford, Margaret Baker, and Eileen Bagoy. Second row: Anna Savola, Marjorie Balhizer, Betty Kruger, Myrtle Morton, and Vivian Stoddard.

Just as Cecil Sly took on conducting duties in addition to his responsibilities as superintendent of schools, the teachers in the high school typically were asked to teach more than one subject. Miss Cuthbertson found herself in front of science classes, holding up beakers and test tubes, in

besides your majors. So, I kept one lesson ahead of the class. Some of the boys got quite interested and they would ask questions I didn't know the answers to. I'd say, 'Well, you know, you are just going to confuse everybody by getting ahead. Let's just wait and take it as it comes in the book.'"

After school social activities centered around dinner or a movie. The Merchant's Café was one of Lorene's favorite restaurants. There were several others doing a thriving business, since the miners and trappers coming into town would frequent them. Some of the local people could be found at Russell Merrill's home, an apartment on H Street, where his wife played the piano, the only baby grand piano in town that Lorene knew of then. "I was often invited there to play the piano so that everyone could dance after dinner. The floor was linoleum – with extra wax."

Her apartment was upstairs in a building on the corner of Fourth Avenue and G Street. Two blocks away, on the corner of Fourth and E, was Hewitt's Drug Store,

Lorene and George Valaer in 1929 - "We're on 9th Avenue where we walked out to see one of those strange things, an airplane. That was a real novelty. I remember some of the planes landing head-first into the snow on the strip."

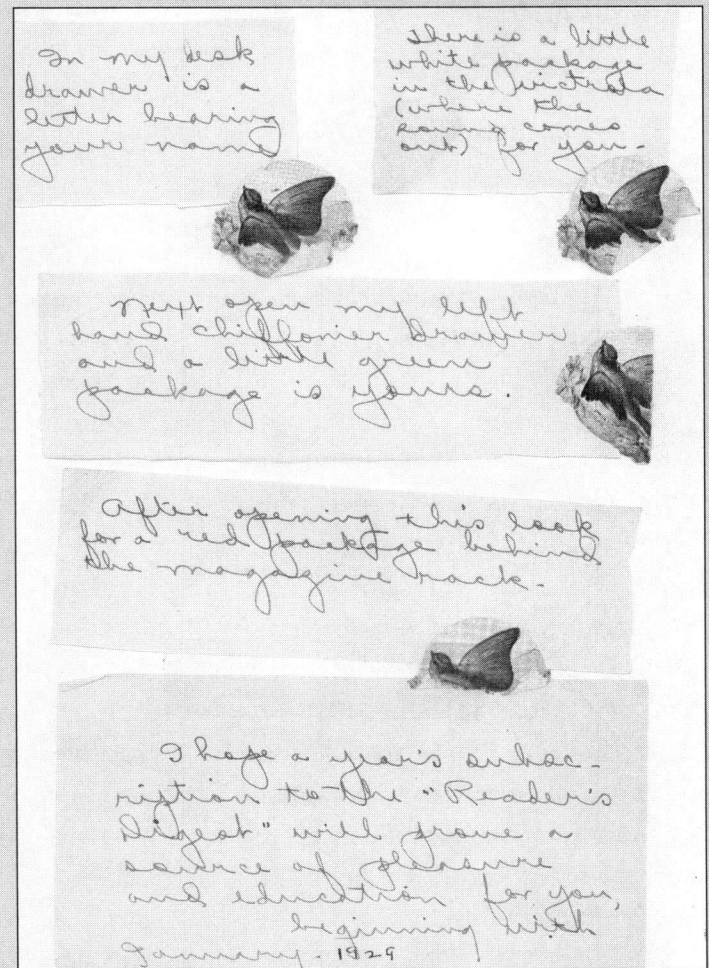

Lorene gave George a gift subscription to the Readers' Digest for his birthday — January 6, 1929.

owned by Denny and Nell Hewitt. "That's where the kids would go after school. They had a fountain there and the kids gathered there for a soda or to buy records." Lorene had brought the complete works of Shakespeare north with her, and on the weekends some of the high school students gathered in her apartment to read them out loud together. "It was something else for them to do and became quite popular." At age 23 she found it easy to establish rapport with her high school students. "I was just a few years older than many of them."

After she began teaching in Anchorage, one of her students and his father invited Lorene to dinner. The Valaer family consisted of this father and his only son. The mother had died from cancer, after the family had moved from Switzerland. The father spoke mostly German. George Valaer was a high school senior, and grew very close to Lorene. A star on the high school basketball team, he was also interested in acting and had one of the lead roles in *Miss Cherry Blossom*. ("George is always good," the newspaper review had stated, praising him for his role as villain and stock broker in the operetta.) He hoped to be a dentist.

June 26, 1929. That is a date that Lorene will never forget. Life has large moments, turning points. When the phone rang in her apartment that day, life would take a permanent turn. "It was a friend calling from the Anchorage Hotel where she had been playing bridge. The word had just come by telephone that there was an accident on the railroad tracks north of Nenana where George had been working as a surveyor for the summer." George Valaer had been killed, along with his co-worker.

Lorene had known that June that she would be going "Outside," returning to Kansas to teach in a town nearer her parents. George had been planning to attend a dental school in Minnesota. The impact of his loss would be permanent. "I was his surrogate mother and confidante and best friend. His loss taught me to value every moment — every friendship," Lorene states. "You never know how many more moments you are going to get."

She vividly remembers the moment she got the news. "I dropped the receiver in complete shock and looked out the window. Jack Harrison was coming across the street. I had had two dates with him. Jack was coming to my apartment to share the same news. He would be a big help to me, dealing with this loss."

Chapter Eight
Time "Outside"
A Short Break in the Alaskan Chord

Lorene had met Jack Harrison shortly before she left Alaska to take on her new teaching assignment in Pawnee Rock, Kansas. He was a big game guide, along with his friend Rusty Annabell, who wrote about his hunting experiences for the national outdoor magazine, *Field and Stream*. Rusty was dating Rica Niemi, the young teacher Lorene had met, carrying her violin onto the steamer in Juneau.

"Rica and Rusty were going to the movies," Lorene remembers. "Jack called and asked for me, wanting to know if I would like to double date with Rica and Rusty." That date was followed by an outing much more adventuresome than a movie. "Jack hired Frank Dorbandt, a pilot and World War I flying ace, to take us up in a plane on the longest day of the year, June 21, 1929." (It was just a few days before George would die.)

Lorene continues, "Everyone knew Frank. The plane was a single engine, two-seater, so I sat on Jack's lap, complete with my scarf, helmet and goggles since it was an open cockpit airplane. We took off from what is now the Park Strip, the only air field there was here at that time."

That date definitely got her attention. "Jack had asked Frank to do 'something interesting,' so we found ourselves hanging on and

Mostly Music

hanging on while the plane did a few side slips."

That July, Lorene left Anchorage, keeping her promise to her parents to teach in Kansas. Jack followed her Outside, coming to Kansas to visit her for Christmas, 1929. "He had planned to go to college in Denver, Colorado to get a degree in chemical engineering. Only a few months after we had met, Jack 'popped the question.' I said 'yes,' and we were married at Grand Lake on top of a mountain near Denver on July 3, 1930." Looking back, Lorene states wistfully, "We really hadn't known each other long enough."

The newly married couple bought a house in Colorado, but financially tough times were just ahead. "Little did we realize in 1930 that the Great Depression was really upon us," Lorene states. "We couldn't make the payments, and eventually lost the house." In 1931, Lorene and Jack decided to move back to Sterling, Kansas and live with Lorene's parents, while Jack took a job selling insurance, trying to make ends meet. On February 15, 1932, their daughter was born in that Sterling home. Baby Margaret Lee came to be known as Pegge.

The new family stayed with Lorene's parents for six months

Rica Niemi and Lorene each peek out from behind an "Alaska Big Fish." They both worked at Emard Cannery for three weeks in 1929, "just for the heck of it, at the end of the school year," according to Lorene.

Lorene Harrison

Jack Harrison and Lorene Cuthbertson's wedding announcement in 1930 - "To all our special friends."

Three of Anchorage's first pilots - (right to left): Frank Dorbandt, Alonzo Cope, Russ Merrill - 1929.

July 3, 1930 - Lorene and Jack's wedding day — the wedding took place at Grand Lake on top of a mountain near Denver, CO.

Pegge in Denver, November, 1933, about age 2 - Lorene had made her little rose-colored satin coat and hat.

Lorene and Jack's home in Denver, where they lived when the Great Depression hit.

Sterling, Kansas - the house where Margaret Lee (Pegge) was born on February 15, 1932.

after Pegge's birth, then moved to Denver. Along with so many other families during the Depression, they struggled financially. "Jack was making $45 a month," Lorene recalls, "and our rent was $15 a month. Banks were going down everywhere, there were many suicides – no one had any money. Friends helped us, especially friends in Denver, the Niblos, who had a grocery store. They visited us every Sunday, and gave us what they couldn't sell in their store – overripe vegetables and fruits. I could never thank them enough. Many years later, during better times, they would visit us in Alaska. I remember one Denver night we woke up so hungry we couldn't sleep. We had one piece of bread and an onion. We made an onion sandwich. We always saw that little Pegge got what she needed."

Jack's stepfather, "Dad Sullivan," had moved his young family from Colorado to Anchorage when Jack was only 11 years old. Jack's mother, Bessie Lee, had died recently, and Dad Sullivan — Daily Sullivan — was still in Anchorage when the Depression hit. "Dad Sullivan encouraged us to move back to Alaska," Lorene says. "He offered to pay our way up. Jack and I both knew we loved Alaska. We had struggled so in Colorado, we looked on Alaska as 'the Promised Land.' And Dad Sullivan could use help raising two children, Doris and Charles, then in high school." Lorene could be "the woman of the house," he suggested.

72

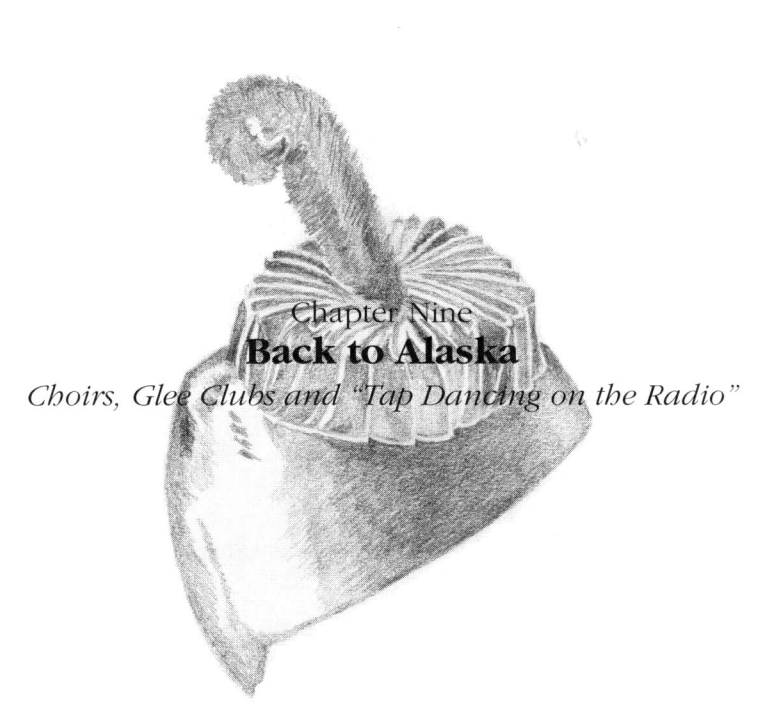

Chapter Nine
Back to Alaska
Choirs, Glee Clubs and "Tap Dancing on the Radio"

*I*t was in January of 1934, then, that Lorene and Jack, with daughter Pegge, not quite two years old, packed up their few belongings, caught the train from Colorado to Seattle, took the boat up the coast, and returned "home" to Alaska. To save money, Jack came at the steerage rate of $10, Lorene paid the first class rate of $64, and she remembers little Pegge "traveled at minimal fare – if at any cost."

Lorene continues, "We didn't have any money at all. That was such a big concern, as you can imagine, even though we had a home to go to and Jack would be working with the railroad. That was lots more than many people had in those Depression days." Jack had put aside his plans, begun in Colorado, of finishing his degree in engineering, and focused on supporting his family.

Lorene did not have to puzzle over filling her time. Keeping Dad Sullivan's rented two-story log-house was a monumental task, by any standards. His home sat on E Street, one block from Kimball's store, or where the Performing Arts Center Town Park is today. As Lorene puts it, she would soon find herself "looking after two men and two high school children — Jack's half-sister, Doris, and half-brother, Charles — and two babies." In addition to Daily's two children, toddler Pegge would be joined by baby sister,

Mostly Music

The Government (Railroad) Hospital on 2nd Avenue, where Carol Anne was born on November 19, 1934. (It's no longer there.)

Carol Anne at 6 months.

Pegge on the steamship Yukon in 1934 - The family was moving back to Alaska from Denver. "The boat trip from Seattle to Seward took about 7 days then, with virtually no tourists on board."

Lorene Harrison

Carol Anne, born on November 19, 1934, in the railroad-owned hospital on Second Avenue.

Lorene remembers days full of baking bread, using a plunger in a bath tub to wash clothes and sheets for six, and cooking on a coal stove. "We were as poor as church mice," she states. "I couldn't have taught in the public school fulltime if I'd wanted to. In those days, a married woman couldn't have a teaching contract." To help the family financially, she did some substitute teaching at Anchorage Public School — still the only school in town, took in some sewing, made all the family's clothing, and soon began giving voice and piano lessons. "I was so pleased to have a piano," Lorene states. Jack's mother had left an old upright piano in the house. Her first music students were mostly adults. She had a class of six high school girls who walked the three blocks to

Elks Club entertainment hits the 1930s "quiet town" on a Saturday night - Here Lorene trained a festive troupe bringing Mexico to Alaska at the Elks Club. The troupe members are (left to right, front row) Clarice Telder, Georgia Warriner, Charlotte Leer, Mildred Kirkpatrick, Bea Burgan, Peggy Snight, Hilda Corey. (Second row) Blanche Fousek, Agnes Mills, Bill Kinsell, Bob Abernethy, Wayne Priem, Lorene. (Third row) Betty Harlacher, Hank Lally, Cleo Simonds, Elly Snight, Mary Lou Slade.

her home after school, and paid 50 cents for an hour's lesson.

"Besides my music lessons, I remember only Ken Loughlin teaching piano and organ, at the Empress Theatre. There were maybe 4,000 people in town by then, and that was about it for music lessons."

There were just three churches in town in 1934. The Presbyterian Church on Fifth Avenue and F was one of them. Lorene had been a Presbyterian all her life, so soon after returning to Anchorage, she began to attend services there. It didn't take long for her music abilities to be discovered by the congregation, and she was approached to become the music director. With Lorene at the helm, the Presbyterian Church Choir played a major part in planting seeds in the musical history of Anchorage from then on.

"When I began to direct, there were just six or eight choir members, standing up in the front of the congregation," Lorene recalls. "I loved those beginnings. I felt as long as someone could stand up there, and encourage others, they could belong. There were no auditions." As membership grew, the choir occasionally outnumbered the congregation. There were no church organs in town. The one organ Lorene knows of at that time was in the Empress Theatre. Robert and Evangeline Atwood had moved to Anchorage in 1936. "Bob sang in the choir," Lorene recalls, "and Evangeline would play the piano for both the church and the choir. Elsie Sogn was one of the early choir members."

Carol Anne and the family pet, "Susie" Harrison

Lorene Harrison

Carol Anne, about 2 years old.

Winter of 1936 - Pegge and Carol are by their little white house, with the school in the background. They are wearing snow suits Lorene made out of their grandfather's winter coats.

Carol Anne in front of "the too small red house" on the corner of 6th and G streets, near the location of today's Westmark Hotel.

Summer of 1939 - The family is now in a larger home at the corner of 6th and I, where La Mex is today, then "a nice residential area." Carol Anne (on left) is 4 and Pegge is 6. Lorene recalls, "I sometimes made dresses alike for my daughters, but in different colors."

Lorene remembers the Anchorage of the 1930s as "very quiet." "People didn't make too much noise. They were just trying to scratch out a living. But, oh, goodness, did we love to dance." The Elks Club was the scene of Saturday night dances, featuring waltzes and fox trots, with a small orchestra playing. Lorene remembers that the saxophone player was Eugene Smith, brother-in-law of Rica Niemi, or Rica Swanson, the violin-carrying young woman Lorene had met on the steamer in 1928. There were lots of traveling salesmen, coming to town in those days, "selling everything from spices to pickles. They'd get dates, and go dancing."

Sadness struck the family in the fall of 1935. The children of Dad Sullivan, Doris and Charles, had gone "to the states" for college when Dad Sullivan died suddenly, in a fall while working on the Alaska Railroad. After his death, in 1936, the young family — Lorene, Jack, Pegge, and Carol Anne — moved to a little red house on the corner of Seventh and G streets (behind the location of what is today the Westmark Hotel). Lorene remembers the home as being so small that the two little girls, Pegge and Carol Anne, shared a big windowed-closet as a bedroom, not too far from a big potbellied stove in the living room. "I often had nightmares of fire," Lorene remembers. In 1938, the family moved to the corner of 6th and I, where the La Mex restaurant is today. The family rented this home for seven years – Lorene remembers it as "a nice two-bedroom home in a residential area" — until the owner sold it in 1945.

By 1935, Lorene had spotted lots of untapped and unorganized musical talent, beyond her responsibilities as director of the First Presbyterian Church Choir. She organized first a Women's Community Glee Club, and then a Men's Community Glee Club. "When the men saw how much fun the women were having, they asked me to organize them too," Lorene recalls. She joined the two together for a Christmas program in 1936. "There were about 25 women members and 20 men. We rehearsed at the Presbyterian Church, and sometimes at my home."

A banner headline from the *Anchorage Daily Times* of December 10, 1937, reads "More Than Half a Hundred to Sing Tonight," referring to the combined glee clubs' second annual Christmas music concert. It was held at the Elks Hall with Lorene as director and Helen Welch as accompanist. Sub-headlines read, "Anchorage To Hear Notable Choral Pieces — Two Glee Clubs and Famed Soloist Give Talents to the

Public." The clipping reports that the guest soloist was Mrs. R. L. Works (Doris, wife of Dr. Works, an ENT — ear, nose and throat specialist — and one of the few doctors in town then), and that president of the Women's Glee Club, Mrs. Frank L. Reed, had overseen the ticket sales. Almost 200 tickets had been sold by the day of the performance, "with strong indications that a packed house would greet the choral clubs" that night at the Elks Hall.

Rave reviews followed. The next day, the front page of the paper reported, "High Praise Given Glee Clubs and Leader." "With the Elks Hall filled to capacity, a more appreciative audience would be most difficult to gather in one place." The article goes on to state, "A tremendous ovation greeted Lorene Harrison as she stepped upon the rostrum, it being necessary to bow several times before starting the program. Dressed in a charming light delicate blue tinted evening gown, she was resplendent as conductress."

1936, the first Fur Rendezvous — Lorene, as director of music and entertainment, organized a Fur Fashion Show at the Elks Hall. (Lorene is first on the left in front.)

One of Lorene's favorite stories comes from this performance, causing a swell of laughter to this day, in her telling of it. The story made the next day's newspaper, told by an equally bemused reporter, Maurice Sharp. Dr. Heitmeyer, one of Dr. Works' co-workers and friends, had been ushered in to a front-row seat for the sold-out concert. The paper reports, "The audience, intent on listening to the guest soloist, was shaken severely by the sudden crash in the very front row directly in front of Mrs. Works. A ripple of snickers passed through the hall." Dr. Heitmeyer's chair had collapsed beneath him during her second solo. The report continues, "Perhaps the greatest strain of the occasion fell on Mrs. Works who, showing the fine stage presence that brought her fame in the States and Europe, continued her number without apparent difficulty. Mrs. Works turned and sang to the balcony, with eyes closed." In similar sporting fashion, Dr. Heitmeyer is quoted as saying, "I fell for her and am proud of it. Her fine voice knocked me out of the chair."

Pegge on her first day of kindergarten - Lorene organized the first public school kindergarten in Anchorage, circulating a petition in 1938.

Music, led by Lorene, was obviously bringing joy to the town. She had also jumped into involvement with the first Fur Rendezvous winter celebration, in 1936. Lorene was named director of music and entertainment. In its beginnings, furs played a prominent part in the Rondy festivities; Lorene organized a Fur Fashion Show, with singing, as a main event. She remembers being paid $10 to arrange the show, to be held in the Elks Hall. As a backdrop for the show, Lorene had Jeannie Laurence, wife of famed Alaskan artist Sydney Laurence, create a big background painting – mountains, cabins, and northern lights. Early photos of these Fur Rendezvous fashion shows show women standing proudly, furs draped over their shoulders, hats – often plumed — perched on heads. This 1936 event is just the beginning of another of Lorene's major interests and community contributions. From 1936 on, she estimates that she arranged over 500 fashion shows in Anchorage.

By 1938, it had become obvious that

there was enough support for music in the town to explore the possibility of bringing up a guest artist "from the States." On October 13, 1938 in the Empress Theatre, the choir of the First Presbyterian Church sponsored the appearance of Mrs. Margaret Bowen, a soprano soloist from Seattle. The choir performed several pieces with her, accompanied by Mrs. Atwood at the piano. Lorene herself wrote of the event in the newspaper the next day. "Practically unanimous approval was voiced, in this, the first attempt in Anchorage to sponsor and support an outside musical artist, and it is felt that if such a venture is repeated, many more than 300 persons will turn out to take advantage of an evening of extraordinary musical delight."

With so much involvement in the community, it could be easy to lose sight of the fact that Lorene had two little daughters that she considered her primary interest. By 1938, Pegge was six years old and Carol Anne was four. Lorene spotted more uncharted territory in her home town. There was no public school kindergarten. "I had gone to kindergarten," Lorene reports. "It was very fulfilling, and I wanted my daughters to have that same important, nice experience. There were now enough children in town the right age for kindergarten to be possible." Discovering that no one was working toward the establishment of a kindergarten, Lorene, in typical fashion, decided to champion the effort herself. "I went to the mayor with a petition. Once I got things started, everybody wanted this."

Carol Anne and Pegge in Sunday outfits, ready for church.

A newspaper clipping from 1938 tells of her progress. "A petition asking for the establishment of a kindergarten class in the Anchorage Public Schools during the school year 1938-39, is being circulated among parents. Mrs. Jack Harrison, who started the petition, said it was prompted when it was learned that there is no provision at present for using the new kindergarten quarters in the new grade school to be built this summer. 'I have a list of 49 children who will be of age to enter the first grade next fall,' Mrs. Harrison said. 'Since making the list, I have learned of several more. It will be most difficult for the first grade teachers to take on such a big class of pupils who have never had any school training.'"

Pegge and Carol Anne on Easter Sunday - "Hats were already important to the women of the family," Lorene states

The article went on to show the growth in very young children in the city. There were 41 first-graders in 1934, 37 in 1935, 50 in 1936, and 51 in 1937. Lorene made copies of her petition available at two local stores, Vaara's and the Anchorage Grocery. Her efforts were successful, and public kindergarten began in Anchorage that fall.

With care for her daughters in mind, Lorene often brought music responsibilities to her home, a kind of early version of today's home-based business. But for Lorene, music was always passion first, and a business, second. Both Pegge and Carol Anne remember the home of their childhood as always being full of music, guests, and home-cooked food. Looking back, Pegge states, "It was not a matter of *if* we would have company, but *who* it would be." Pegge remembers she and Carol Anne would go to the kitchen and close the door when her mother taught voice lessons at home, but they were always able to hear the sessions.

Seeds of the *Messiah* performances that have become tradition in Anchorage were planted by Lorene around 1940. She played a London version of the *Messiah* on records in the high school auditorium for the music committee of the Anchorage Women's Club. What Lorene terms a "unique" performance method evolved. The records played the choruses from the *Messiah*, but local people took the solo parts as they came up on the records. She remembers that when the recording came

called *Musical Courier*, in an attempt to dispel the concept of Alaska as a land with no arts. The letter follows, providing us with a kind of state-of-the-musical-arts verification for that time.

The "Etude Magazine" published an article written by Lorene about music in Alaska in 1942, including a photo of the First Presbyterian Choir, which Lorene directed for 27 years.

to the tenor solos, Herb Cochran took the part; when the soprano solos occurred, Lorene took them; and Marion Barnes sang the contralto solos. There was also a baritone soloist.

By 1940, Lorene had great pride in the quality of music performances evolving in Anchorage, and wanted to tell the Outside world about them. She wrote a letter, dated December 28, 1941, to a national publication,

For some years I have read the Musical Courier from cover to cover. One who is away from large musical centers appreciates the current news of music and the artists in this way. Although, to New Yorkers, Alaska may seem the end of the world, we are by no means completely isolated from the arts. True, we have not the opportunity to see opera nor hear Metropolitan artists, but we do make our own music and derive definite pleasure from it. I dare say you would be amazed at the number of fine vocal and symphony records in the homes of Alaskans, too.

For cultural entertainment, music

holds the spotlight for winter activities in Anchorage. I firmly believe there is no place belonging to the U.S.A. with a population of 3,500 where more above-the-average talent may be found. I have lived here for seven years, having directed the choir of the First Presbyterian Church all that time, both a Women's and Men's Glee Club two years, responding to calls for trios, quartets, solos, radio programs over our local radio station KFQD, and at present have a vocal class of twenty students. This, you understand, is just a 'side line,' as keeping house for my husband and two young daughters is my very real occupation.

I mention the above so that you will realize I have been in a position to see the interest and progress made in music in that period. One noticeable thing is the extreme fluctuation in personnel in musical organizations. Among the fifty-some persons turning out for rehearsal for our Christmas cantata this year, only six have been in the choir for more than three years. As a special feature, Jayne Rullman, harpist, played a group of Christmas numbers and accompanied her husband, F. J. Chesarek, as he sang Schubert's "Ave Maria."
    Musically yours,
    Mrs. Jack (Lorene) Harrison

A note of prophesy followed in the magazine, from the editor. He wrote, "Perhaps some enterprising concert executive may soon see a profitable opportunity for extending the itineraries of his artists to this northern principality. Now that plane jumps are in the everyday schedule of our swiftly traveling musicians, it would not be altogether beyond the possibilities to combine such a visit with one to Western Canada." (This hints of what would indeed become — the Music Trail, evolving into today's Anchorage Concert Association.)

A year later, in 1942, Lorene again took up her pen to tell the world about music in Alaska, this time addressing The *Etude Magazine*. The article included a photo of the choir of the First Presbyterian Church at its 1941 Christmas concert, 52 members depicted. It includes much of the same information as her *Musical Courier* letter. Some of her comments follow.

I lay no claim to being a professional. I was a small-town music supervisor, coming here first thirteen years ago in that capacity. My paramount aim is to assist the singers in having fun in singing, and making it a real pleasure and outlet for themselves. Alaska is a 'working people's' country, and the women in the chorales are housewives, like myself, or working girls. Anchorage is deluged with numerous and varied organizations; thus one night a week, except when concentrating on Christmas or Easter music, is our rehearsal time.

To raise money for our Music Department, our choir gives an annual secular concert in November. Because of the influx of people here due to National Defense projects, we gave the concert two evenings and cleared $225 at 55 cents admission price. The audiences are most appreciative indeed, and there is always the urge for 'more.' More than one tourist has commented that we could put many a larger choir in the States to shame. We have some fine outstanding talent at present, and how noticeable it is that the artists with real music in their souls are both ready and willing to assist whenever asked! We, who have been here for some years, so deeply appreciate their generous attitude.

In our thirst for a musical outlet, we not only find joy in singing, but also find ourselves growing into a close companionship which is so essential for every individual who finds himself so far away from former home and friends. Maybe we love to sing because we enjoy each other so much, or perhaps vice versa. Anyway, I am so proud of the work my groups have done that I am enclosing a picture taken last year when we sang our Christmas Cantata. Last Easter we took great pride in singing Dubois "The Seven Last Words of Christ."

Pegge and Carol Anne in the winter of 1940, with dog Susie - Both share many happy memories of growing up in Anchorage in the 1930s and 40s.

In addition to conducting, Lorene was also involved in arranging music. In 1941, Lorene composed the first four-part arrangement of what would become Alaska's beloved state song, the *Alaska Flag Song*. The flag was designed in 1927, the year before Lorene first came to Anchorage to teach in the public school. Its young designer, Benny Benson, became one of Lorene's friends. Inspired by the flag's design, state she had left in 1936, put Drake's words to music in 1938. Lorene's four-part arrangement of the music made its debut as part of the 1941 Fur Rendezvous celebration, at the outdoor coronation of the Fur Rendezvous queen by Brig. General Simon B. Buckner, Jr., commanding general of the Alaska Defense Command.

Lorene's nephew, Bob, Jr. (Bob Wyatt), was married in Anchorage on September 23, 1942. The wedding took place in the first little Presbyterian Church. Lorene was matron of honor and Jack gave the bride, Elda, away.

Marie Drake, Assistant Commissioner of Education for the Territory of Alaska, had written a poem titled Alaska's Flag in 1935. A public school choral director in Nebraska, Elinor Dusenbury, homesick for the

The newspaper the following day, February 19, 1941, described the events leading up to the performance of the *Flag Song*. First there were young ice skaters, followed by children performing "a lovely penguin dance," then a "delightful sled dance," then vocals by a men's quartet. The article reads, "The men, with four girls, joined in singing *Alaska's Flag*, a new song published recently. A beautiful Alaska flag of the Pioneer lodge was unfurled as they sang. Most of the accompaniments were by Mrs. Jack Harrison." (Lorene's four-part vocal arrangement of the *Alaska Flag Song* was also sung by the Community Chorus at the grand opening of the 4th Avenue Theater in 1946.)

Lorene's daughters, Pegge and Carol

Lorene Harrison

Anne, both remember these early years of their childhood in Anchorage as halcyon days, full of song, tap dance lessons, 4th of July parades, house guests, roller skating on the wooden sidewalk along Sixth Avenue, ice skating on the ball park in the winters, sledding at the end of Fourth Avenue down the hill to the inlet, and playing near the railroad tracks in Bootleggers Cove in the summers. They remember progressive dinners, going house-to-house in the snow to the homes of family friends. There were also visits from much older cousins — Bob, Jr., their aunt Nina's son; and Louise, their uncle Will's daughter. Both would marry in Anchorage and live here for a time.

One of Pegge's fondest memories comes from her childhood at age 10, in 1942. (Married in 1953 to Joseph Vielbig, today she is Pegge Vielbig.)

Pegge tells her story. "I took dance lessons from Gertrude Mulcahy — Mulcahy Park is named for her husband. She had been a performer in New York and had begun a little dance studio for children. Mrs. Mulcahy also started a Junior Theater Guild and put on little plays. The first radio station in town, KFQD, began broadcasting in 1924. I remember that in about 1940, it was on the air every evening from 5 p.m.

Pegge dressed up to be in the 4th of July parade, as a bride on a wedding cake prop. Don Glass was her groom. (He was the son of an early Alaska pilot.)

to 9 p.m., and on Friday and Saturday nights, they often had local entertainment. Mrs. Mulcahy would bring in a group of little girls, members of the Junior Theater Guild, and we would put on our plays, sing, or recite poems on the radio for about 15 minutes. But the performance I remember most clearly today, was one evening when we were featured — tap dancing on the radio."

Many of Carol Anne's childhood memories center around company in the home and the food Lorene prepared. (Carol Anne was married would take leftover cake, make a clear white sauce with vanilla to pour over it, and we'd have 'blanc mange.' I still make some of mother's recipes today."

Sometimes Lorene would make a dinner featuring moose that Jack had

Lorene's niece, Louise, married Bill Frederick in 1943 in Anchorage. Once again, Aunt Lorene was the matron of honor.

in 1956 to Bob Dodd.) "We had so many guests," Carol Anne remembers, "that mother kept a little black book of who had been to dinner, what date, and what she had served them. She made clover leaf rolls in muffin tins by the thousands. Mother hunted and brought home. Carol Anne remembers those moose, hanging beside the house. "Dad would go out and hack off a chunk of moose. We'd take it inside, and mother would stew it up." Jack would also go hunting "right where the Pioneers' Home is today," according to Carol Anne. "Dad would come home with rabbit and ptarmigan he'd got there."

The little black notebook still exists, providing family history as well as food notes. For example, on February 15, 1942, Pegge's tenth birthday, her mother served fried chicken, mashed potatoes, beet Jello, her famous rolls, and vegetables, along with the birthday cake she'd made.

Both Pegge and Carol Anne attended the one grade school then in town, on the same block as the high school, where the Performing Arts Center is today, between Fifth and Sixth avenues, and F and G streets. Pegge remembers a "horrible blizzard" that occurred when she was in the third grade. "Normally we would walk home for lunch in the middle of the school day. That day mother came from home through the storm with a thermos of hot soup for me and my third grade teacher, Mrs. Viola Porter."

Creeping into the newspaper clippings from the 1930s and early 1940s, full of entertainment news centered on the Elks Club

"The Happy Harrison Four" in 1940 in their 6th and I Street home. "Jack was an engineer for the government railroad, all through the war years, so was out on the road a great deal."

and the Presbyterian Church, come notes of the threat of war. Also, among the happy childhood stories of both Carol Anne and Pegge, ominous memories of preparations for World War II begin to appear. An article dated April 17, 1942 tells of a minstrel show, backed by a chorus directed by Lorene, in the "large high school auditorium" keeping the overflow crowd "in spasms of laughter." Lower, in that same newspaper column, the following headline appears, "Blackout Now Is from 4 to 6." The alert states simply, "Blackout hours were moved back 30 minutes by official announcement today at Fort Richardson. The new blackout period to be observed in Anchorage will be from 4 o'clock in the morning to 6 o'clock in the morning."

At home during the blackouts, layers of newspapers were taped over the windows, or heavy curtains were drawn. "We were allowed only flashlights to see where we were going," Lorene remembers, "and both street lights and car headlights were forbidden." Air raid warning whistles would blow unexpectedly - false alarms, but terrifying.

At school, from the time she was about 9 until she was 13 years old, Pegge remembers drills in which the children were taught to "take cover" under their desks. There were competitions among the classrooms to see which students could put the most 50-cent stamps in coupon books, to purchase war bonds. "Much about those war days is still a hurtful puzzle to me," Pegge states. "Sammy Kimura, who was 9, was my friend. One day he wasn't in school. I didn't understand why he had to leave school — why he and his family were placed in an internment camp."

Once the war began, the Harrisons dug a fox hole in their backyard, as did many families in the city. The war would have a profound impact on Anchorage. Hundreds of soldiers were brought into town, and the population increased from 7,700 in 1941 to 25,000 in 1943. The women and children were asked to leave the city, but the Harrisons decided to stay. There would be no formal performances by the men's or women's glee clubs during the war years; the Fur Rendezvous winter celebrations were temporarily disbanded.

Despite the hardships, Lorene looks back on these war days as some of the most fulfilling and happiest of her life. And they were full of music.

Chapter Ten
The War Years - The Music Plays On, Cheering Soldiers' Souls
"My work was needed."

"It seems odd, doesn't it, that the war years were some of the happiest of my life," Lorene states, reflecting back to the early to mid-1940s. "I felt that I was accomplishing something important – that my work was needed."

In 1942, Lorene was appointed music director and afternoon hostess for the local USO, United Service Organization. "The director of the USO asked me to assume these duties. It became the largest USO in the country, although we were considered 'overseas' at that time. Security was incredibly tight. All the mail was opened and censored." The USO was a log building, built by the soldiers, its base constructed from trees cut down at Fort Richardson (located where Elmendorf Air Force Base is today). Situated near the corner of Fifth and G streets, where the Westmark Hotel is today, it was complete with bowling alleys; a food canteen full of homemade cookies, cakes and sandwiches donated by the community; a big lounge; writing tables; basement with a pool table; and photography dark rooms for "our men in uniform."

A 1942 newspaper clipping from the *Anchorage Daily Times* states, "Appointment of Mrs. Jack Harrison to the post of assistant hostess at the USO, to be in charge of music, was announced today by Forrest Knapp, director. Mrs. Harrison has taken an active interest in USO work for some time and has assisted in organizing choruses and other musical events on the program. In her work, Mrs. Harrison will devote a major portion of her time to the musical work with soldiers and she will act as assistant hostess to Miss Marguerite Conrady."

Music filled Lorene's life through the war years, and she saw to it that it also filled the USO. It didn't take her long to bring on the melodies. A clipping in the paper, just a short time after Lorene's appointment to these new duties, declares:

"Reports today indicated that folks were having a 'swell time' at the community sings sponsored at the USO each Sunday evening. As an added attraction, Mrs. Jack Harrison, newly appointed musical director, yesterday organized a music appreciation group which will meet immediately following the 'sing's' on Sunday nights.

"Cake and coffee were served last evening by the Business and Professional Women's Club. Hostesses included the Mesdames A.W. Coutts, John Coats, U.S. Hanshew, J.B. Gottstein, W.A. Smith, Alfred Balls, Charan Baldwin, Robert Bragaw, Ed Barber, Frank Pauls, and W.M. Cuddy."

Other groups that acted as hostesses for events at the USO included the Anchorage Women's Club, the wives of the Junior Chamber of Commerce, and the Presbyterian Friendly Aid.

Lorene dropped her private music lessons when she added these USO duties to her daily responsi-

Lorene as music director and afternoon hostess at her desk in the USO Log Cabin, where she befriended soldiers far from home-1942.

Lorene Harrison

The USO stage was transformed into the Malamute Saloon, scene of a rowdy "Shooting of Dan McGrew" in 1943 - directed by Lorene.

Lined up and calmed down after the "Shooting" - the cast, with Lorene, "the Lady Known as Lou" (second from the left, back row) - "We had scads of fun!"

Mostly Music

bilities. "But the work combined well with my family responsibilities," she states. "Carol Anne was 8 and Pegge was 10 when I began this work. They could just walk across the street after school to the USO. The soldiers missed their own families and they doted on the girls. They spoiled them with little gifts."

Pegge remembers many of the G.I.'s coming to their house for home-cooked dinners. "Mom was famous for her cooking – especially her hot rolls." One soldier even took to poetry to express his appreciation, writing 'Ode to a Hot Bun' in 1942.

The Lady Known as Lou plays to the USO crowd, 1943. "The three young civilians, sitting, were in the USO Camp Troop, Inc. from New York. They had given a marvelous show at our USO some weeks before, so our manager wanted to get them into the fun. I 'played up' to them, and Dan McGrew (Walter Culver) kept his eyes on me and - being very jealous - would pull me away. The Major sitting in the front row was a good friend of mine, Chaplain Applegate of Alaska Defense Command (head of Alaska chaplains). There was sawdust on the floor, and a Coke bar behind the crowd. Lanterns and candles stuck in liquor bottles were our only lights."

Pegge adds, "She made a cake for them, every day of the war, and always for a G.I.'s birthday. She got lots of handwritten thank you notes from them, something of a lost art," Pegge reflects.

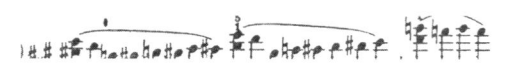

Since the women had been asked to leave the city, there was no women's chorus during the war.

bers. "We'd play the piano – several fellows played very well – and lots of folks gathered around

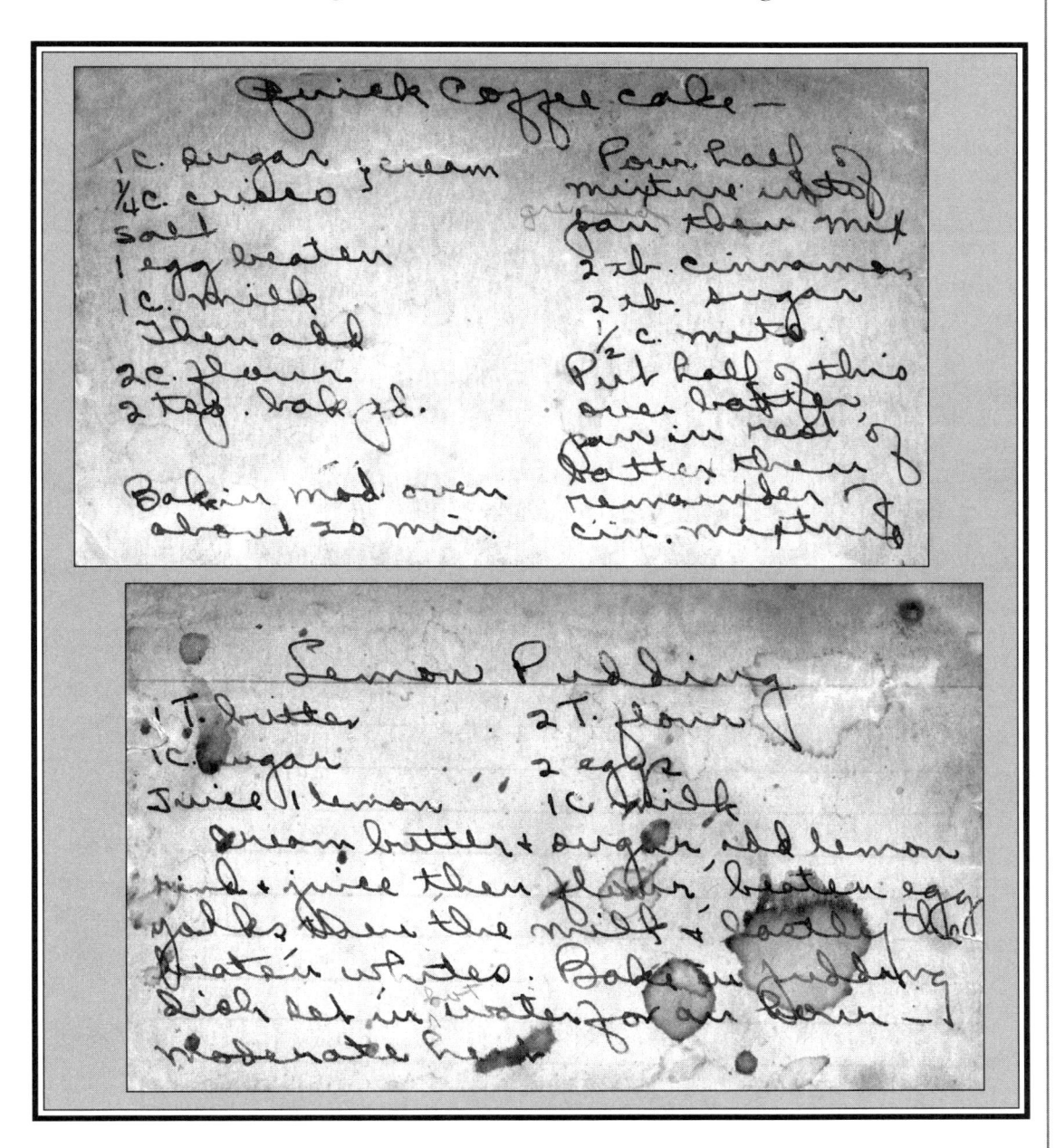

There were no glee clubs either. Music activities at the USO began to fill in these gaps. "The place was always full," Lorene remem-

to sing. If not on duty, they were at the USO." Lorene also began the "You Name It Show," a once-a-month production held in the high school. A November, 1942 clipping in the *Anchorage Daily Times*, reports on these programs.

"Plans for the Thanksgiving evening concert in the high school auditorium under the auspices of the third 'You Name It Show' series, were reaching final stages today, under the direction of Mrs. Jack Harrison.

"Featuring the combined artistry of Simeon Oliver, Alaskan pianist, and the choral group from the Presbyterian church under the direction of Mrs. Jack Harrison, the program promises to be the outstanding musical program to date this season.

"Oliver, composer of some 75 ballads and songs and numerous Aleutian melodies, will present his popular 'native folksongs and folklore' with illustrations of his own on the piano.

"Several choral numbers, violin solos and vocal trio selections from last week's popular Spanish concert given by the Presbyterian choir will be presented on this same program."

The Spanish concert is in reference to a Song Fiesta, presented on November 20, 1942 in the Presbyterian Church as its annual winter concert. The paper's headline the next day read, "Catchy Spanish Airs Presented with Expert Rendering Last Night," and the reviewer stated, "Mrs. Harrison, who has directed the choir for a number of years and who has exhibited an inexhaustible energy in organizing and directing, led the singers through their musical paces to a more than satisfactory conclusion to an evening of delightful musical entertainment." The writer also reported that the annual concerts by the Presbyterian Church choir had

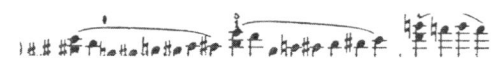

More USO shenanigans - This time it's "A Bicycle Built for Two" - in this case, for Lorene and Ralph Schriner - "I don't know what I was saying to make a face like that! That's Charles Richard at the piano, from the Metropolitan Grand Opera Co."

Lorene Harrison

always drawn a large crowd of music lovers "who anticipate the evenings of fine music presented by a capable chorus and director. The custom of the choir has been to invite local musicians as guest artists and it has been a novelty much enjoyed by concert-goers to hear, on more than one choir program, talented artists in their first appearance in Anchorage."

The newspaper announcement of the third "You Name It Show" continues, "No tickets will be necessary. Admission is free to both the military personnel and civilians. The concert is jointly sponsored by the USO, Jaycees, and Special Services from the fort."

This third "You Name It Show" provided for the first public appearance in Anchorage of Simeon Oliver. A review in the paper the next day, November 27, 1942, written by one Billie Dunkle, commented on the Aleut folk songs collected, recorded and arranged by Simeon Oliver. She wrote of the Russian influence evident in Oliver's *Aleut Lullaby*, *A Christmas Carol*, and *Native Dancer*. Dunkle enjoyed Oliver's "clever, racy patter" as much as his music, stating that Oliver "gave an amusing epitaph on the lost art of piano tuning in Alaska, or perhaps I should say a lament for the lost piano tuner" - aspects of the music scene that can still exist in today's Alaska, especially in the Bush.

Through the USO, big names in the national entertainment field came to town. Hedda Hopper and Ginger Rogers were just two of them, both performing in Anchorage in 1942. Lorene, utilizing another of

Lorene's "You Name It Show" in the high school introduced the work of Simeon Oliver to Anchorage, including his "Aleut Lullaby." Years later, the two meet again.

her ongoing interests and passions, created hats for both of these women. For Hedda, Lorene made a hat featuring a real crab shell. "That was quite a hat," Lorene recalls, laughing. "The crab shell was in the middle. I put sequins on top of the little points on the crab. There was one big feather swooping down her cheek."

Lorene's ability to bring the com-

Mostly Music

munity together in music, to feature nationally known and new local artists, and to cheer the souls of soldiers far from home resulted in an original musical tribute that eventually was sung over and over by grateful members of the military. First entitled "Lorene, the Hostess," it became known more simply as "Hey, Lorene." (Over half-a-century later, Lorene still hears from the "soldier" who wrote it about her.) The song was introduced to the Anchorage community in a *Times* column appearing regularly throughout the war, *News and Previews from USO* (see inset next page).

Word of the song and its popularity

The USO attracted a crowd of young soldiers. "We'd gather around the piano and sing, often learning some new popular music. Several of the fellows played very well."

even made its way back to Sterling, Kansas, Lorene's original hometown, where her parents were still living. The Sterling paper printed excerpts from an *Anchorage Times* USO column in 1943.

"'Hey, Lorene!' That's the title of a new song whose music and lyrics have been written by one of the boys. The reason for this song is the growing recognition of the usefulness of our music lady, Lorene Harrison. Starting last summer with 30 or 40 men, the fireside sing will soon be packing the house. There were 125 there last night.

"Mrs. Harrison's presentation of high-class music at the now established 'Concert Hour' which is 6:30 each Sunday evening did very definitely pack the house. All seats were taken and so was all the standing room. It was a double feature but either part of

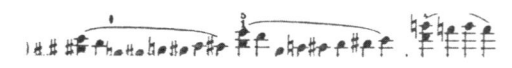

Lorene Harrison

The following column appeared on
November 21, 1942, with the heading —

Nice Lady.

There are so many of them in the world that it seems almost unfair to pick one of them out but we gotta do it on account of a song and lyrics written by Kenneth Fildes of ACS. The song is worthy of publication for it has a very catchy lilt. The words explain the why of USO Hostesses, whether they be dark-eyed Pegs or blue-eyed Lorenes. This is entitled 'Lorene, the Hostess,' a 'cadenza' (whatever that is) in five acts, and we think it is a nice tribute to a very fine woman, Lorene Harrison.

Please don't burden me
With your misery.
I don't want to hear about your woe;
Let me call the gal
Who will be your pal.
She's the worry bird
Of the USO.
So

You got your troubles;
Your watch don't run.
You didn't get a letter;
Your sandwich ain't done.

Some new wolf
Is after your queen.
Don't tell me — Hey, Lorene!

Do you play the oboe like Krysler's fiddle?
So your pants don't fit you.
You're sprung in the middle.

You just heard some news.
I see what you mean.
Don't tell me — Hey, Lorene!

You say you're lonesome,
You wish you were dead.
You think before it's over,
You'll be out of your head.
Well, man, cast your eye
At the girl on the job.
She does the worryin'
For all of the mob.

You think the joint's lovely.
The hostess ain't bad.
You wish that you knew her;
Her eyes are so sad.
Why not tell her,
I'm just part of the scene.
Don't tell me — Hey, Lorene!

Mostly Music

the program would have warranted such a situation.

"Twenty-five joyful voices were raised in song and praise as the fine Presbyterian choir presented a half-hour of splendid Sunday evening music. This splendid organization led by Mrs. Harrison will be welcomed any time."

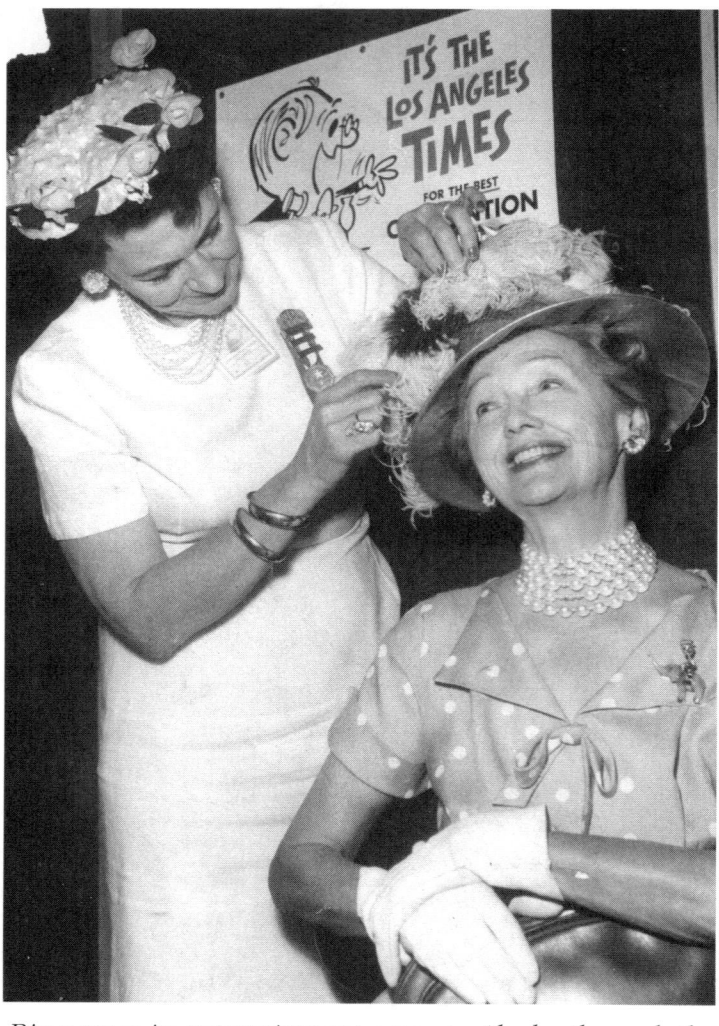

As the afternoon hostess at the USO, Lorene made sure that cakes and coffee were available, gathering local women to help with the baking and serving. These efforts did not go unnoticed by the members of the military, and once again, one of them turned to original poetry to express his gratitude. The tribute was printed in the USO column in the *Times* on December 21, 1942.

"One of the boys who recently enjoyed the cake and coffee served with smiles and friendliness by the ladies at one of the Sunday Afternoon Social Hours expressed his feelings about it thusly –

*'Tho you say it's nothing
To give us boys a treat,
I think I'm right in saying
You ladies can't be beat.*

*You've made us very happy
This Sunday afternoon,*

Big names in entertainment came to Alaska through the USO. Both Hedda Hopper and Ginger Rogers performed in Anchorage in 1942, and Lorene made hats for each of them. "Hedda's was quite a hat. It had a real crab shell in the middle, and sequins on each of the little points of the shell." Years later, in 1966 at a Democratic Convention in L.A., Helen Fisher presented a Lorene hat-creation to Hedda.

And from our hearts we promise,
We won't forget it soon.

Though we're many miles from home,
We've been served such fine cake,
We close our eyes, and Golly!
It's as good as mothers bake.

So our thanks to all you ladies,
You're the grandest folks we know.
We will never forget your kindness
Through the Anchorage USO.'"

In May of 1943, when it was decided to enlarge the USO bustling with activity, Lorene jumped on the opening of the enlarged building as cause for a show and musical celebration. She began something called Bonanza Days, helping to fill in the gap in community activities left when the Fur Rendezvous celebrations were suspended for the war years. The *Anchorage Daily Times* greeted these new festivities with a large banner headline in its edition on May 20, 1943. "Four-Performance 'Bonanza Days' Opens Tomorrow" - and then in a subheading, "Rip-Roarin' Affair To Celebrate Opening of Enlarged Log Cabin." The article began, "Announcement of the complete program for Bonanza Days, marking the opening of the enlarged USO, came today from Mrs. Jack Harrison, in charge of the program. There will be a total of four shows beginning tomorrow night and continuing Saturday night, Sunday afternoon and Sunday night. Officers and enlisted men alike are invited to attend the celebration. The show will be open to the public Sunday afternoon."

It was an immediate success. After its opening, the paper reported that the celebration "opened with a bang at the sawdust floored, candlelit Flora Dora Tavern with songs, dancing, old time jive, and barroom belles who charged a pretty penny in artificial folding money for the pleasure of the dance." There was talk of "merriment that went on unabated," "dancers reaching the heights of dizzy swirling," jovial melodramas, heavy gambling, and rowdy music coming from Ragtime Kid beating at the piano, later disclosed to be Corp. Kenneth Fildes, the composer of the now famous "Hey, Lorene." Others in the cast of characters were later revealed to be Mrs. W. Mulcahy as Diamond Tooth Gertie, Walter Culver as Dangerous Dan McGrew, and Mrs. Jack Harrison as the Lady Known as Lou.

With energy that seemingly never knew how to quit, Lorene continued the Sunday evening musical programs at what was now known as the Friendly Log Cabin. Just one

Mostly Music

week after Bonanza Days, the regular columnist for the *News and Previews from USO* called in a music critic to review one of these weekly performances. Charles Richards, former accompanist for the Metropolitan Opera Company, wrote, "The town of Anchorage can be proud of the local talent evidenced in the concert given Sunday evening in the USO. Soldiers of the post and the civilians present were royally treated to the excellent musical fare by Lorene Harrison, Blanche Fousek, Annette DeLong, and Ruth Hurst….Perhaps the climax of the evening was the vocal trio, Lorene Harrison, Annette DeLong, and Ruth Hurst, accompanied by Miss Fousek. They are definitely 'Hep with the Helium' (in the language of jive). Such a combination is rare indeed and they showed they knew the real understanding of what an ensemble should be….We who are used to

With the Fur Rendezvous temporarily suspended through the war years, Lorene began something called Bonanza Days in 1943, to fill in the entertainment gap. It played to standing-room-only crowds at the Friendly Log Cabin. Standing still for a photo is the entire Bonanza Days "Rip-Roarin'" crew in the USO's Malamute Saloon - 1943. Lorene is in the center of the back row.

high grade musical performances are indeed grateful for the opportunity to hear music by such genuine artists as these. In fact, we say 'Thumbs up!' for more of the same."

The Bonanza Days were repeated in 1944, reportedly to record crowds. According to a newspaper report, "Over 3000 visited the USO went with a double mission — to see her family and her ailing father there, and to contact on her trip Outside many families of the servicemen stationed in Anchorage. "Communications Outside were very difficult during the war. Many families had heard not at all from their Anchorage servicemen. I was given lots of phone numbers by

The "Mixed USO Chorus" - men and women - 1943 - "By late 1943, the women were coming back to town. They'd been requested to leave at the beginning of the war. Boy, were the men happy to have them back - and everyone wanted to sing!"

during the reenactment of the golden days of '98, as turn-away crowds made their way to the Friendly Log Cabin. The astounding total of 1828 sourdough pancakes was served to hungry guests." (This, from the Sourdough Sentinel section of a Seattle, Washington newspaper, dated August 31, 1944.)

In the spring of 1944, word came to Lorene that her father was ill with pneumonia. Under the auspices of the USO, she was provided with transportation back to Kansas, and many soldiers, to let family know where and how they were," Lorene states. She found that the families "were so very grateful – indeed they were."

Discovering that Lorene had returned to her childhood home, the Sterling, Kansas newspaper reported in April, 1944, "On her short trip to the States, she is contacting wives and mothers, and children of servicemen in Alaska. She is making personal calls on several wives, where she has stopovers, and seeing the babies of these soldiers, who have never been home since their babies were born, and are expecting Mrs. Harrison to bring back a full report, such as color of eyes, and hair, shape of nose, etc. She is making long distance telephone calls to distant points in the United States to give a personal

Lt. Irving Rosvold - "During the war years, he became like a member of our family, so kind to our daughters and to Jack and me."

message to anxious wives and mothers of servicemen in Alaska. Mr. Harrison and their two young daughters remained in Alaska."

Lorene says of this trip, "I loved the work so much. Those were some of the happiest days of my life, reconnecting families."

On her return home to Anchorage in early May, the *Anchorage Daily Times* reported in its headline, "Anchorage Woman Turns Visit Home Into Traveling USO." The article dated May 24, 1944, reads, "When Mrs. Jack Harrison travels, it is virtually a mobile USO proposition. It was learned today after she returned from a visit to her former home in Sterling, Kansas, during which she telephoned more than 50 strangers who had friends among her acquaintances here, and met dozens of former Anchorage residents now in the States. Mrs. Harrison brought back a notebook full of messages for soldiers....From Sterling, Kansas, acting under orders from a soldier, she telephoned a mother in Minneapolis to extend greetings from her son. 'The mother was so surprised and pleased to hear the voice of someone from Alaska that she could hardly talk,' Mrs. Harrison said."

Three of the military chaplains who frequented the USO were Colonel Applegate, Colonel Whipple and Major Wheeler. Lorene remembers, "I often went with them in their jeep to talk to a GI in the hospital who had some kind of problem that it seemed only a woman would understand.

"And my war-years memories would not be complete without mentioning Lt. Irving Rosvold. He more or less became a member of our family during the early 1940s, taking both Pegge and Carol Anne shopping for books or dolls. He, Jack and I went to an open house for the artist, Eustice Ziegler, in 1943 in the old Anchorage Hotel. Oh, I loved one of Ziegler's paintings – but is was $100! It was an original oil painting of snow-covered mountains and a figure of a man leading two horses along a stream. Well, my attraction to that painting didn't go unnoticed by Lt. Rosvold. On our next wedding anniversary, he presented it to us as a gift. I was so thrilled! Irving is living in Oklahoma now, and his daughter relays messages between us."

Chapter Eleven
After the War - Late 1944-1950
Hostessing, Hats, and Helping the Arts
Foundations Set for Major Arts Organizations
(Little Theatre, Concert Association)

It is obvious that Lorene served as much more than music director to the USO during the war years. She became a friend and confidante, a shoulder to lean on, for so many in town that it was logical as the war wound down for her to take on a new, important position serving the community as a whole. In 1944, Charlie Wallulus, president of the Lions Club, approached Lorene with an offer. "He told me that there were so many soldiers wanting to stay in Anchorage at that time, and wanting to bring their families north. But there was really no place for all these families — we were still a tiny little town."

Lorene continues, "Charlie told me the Lions wanted to set up a program to give these soldiers a way to find temporary housing — even if it meant putting up a shack or a tent. He told me, 'You know everybody in town. I'd like to offer you a job as Emergency Housing Bureau Director.' He added that the pay wouldn't be much — $125 a month through the USO – but I just told him I was used to not much pay!"

Lorene set up office in a corner of the Anchorage Hotel, "really just a desk and a phone," and set to work. "I enjoyed my duties tremendously, but it was the hardest work of my life," she admits. "People kept pouring into the city. I had to help them, day and night. Some set up home in tents or shacks. I'd call all over town, trying to find any housing, any available bed." In one year, 1945, she found homes for 2,100 people.

An article in the *Anchorage Daily Times*, August 8, 1945, carried the headline, "People Walk Streets, More Due at Weekend," and the subheading, "Housing Bureau Runs out of Rooms with Biggest Influx in Many Weeks." It reads, in part, "New arrivals in Anchorage walked the streets last night for lack of sleeping accommodations, marking the first time that the Housing Bureau failed to find quarters for everyone.

"Mrs. Jack Harrison, director, issued a plea today for residents to 'come to the rescue' again by listing available rooms, beds, cots, or other facilities for the use of an influx of travelers scheduled for Friday. Mrs. Harrison had received word that 196 persons will arrive in Seward next Friday on the first steamer to come from Seattle in two weeks. Forty-five of them will be brought to Anchorage and placed in Alaska Railroad quarters. The remaining 151 may require sleeping quarters. 'With few exceptions, I had exhausted my list by early evening yesterday and calls continued until after midnight,' Mrs. Harrison said.

"Mrs. Harrison said more than 100 men and their wives are searching for permanent quarters at present. Many of them are scheduled to be 'walking the streets' when the next train arrives if the hotels follow the custom of limiting the use of their rooms to one week.

"The USO opened its lounge to soldiers for use overnight. They slept on the floor, davenports, and in chairs after a train arrived from Whittier during the evening and no other quarters were available."

The critical housing shortage persisted through 1945. In September of that year a huge headline read, "Need New Homes Here for 1,288; Housing Shortage Gets Study." The situation was declared "unprecedented" and "very acute for this city." Lt. General Delos C. Emmons, a commanding general, declared there was a great need to build housing for both civilian and military personnel, and to shift from a war- to a postwar mentality in the town and the territory.

By January of 1946, the urgency seemed to have only increased. The *Times* declared on January 16, 1946 that the critical housing shortage had reached its pinnacle. "It was revealed today that at least 227 families are virtually homeless." These homeless were reportedly living in shacks, hotels, or with friends. It was stated that the Anchorage Housing Authority had on hand 1134 requests for federal housing.

Pioneering as a Woman Business Owner

During the crisis, Lorene took on her characteristic role as adviser and friend, above and beyond her official duties. She became a source of information for the influx of wives and families new to the town. "The women didn't know what they could buy here, nor where," Lorene says. Her desire to help them branched out into another professional opportunity. She started the Anchorage Welcoming Service in March of 1946 — still in existence over 50 years later. "I'd never heard of the Welcome Wagon. I just put together my own original ideas to create the service. I'd get a list from the phone department of the new phones being put in, then find out where that person lived and go make a call."

First she'd collect gifts from local merchants to bring them in a basket – donuts, cold cream, jelly, flowers. "I also had letters of welcome from the Chamber of Commerce and the mayor. People were so grateful! I did that for about three years. For years, I'd run into someone and they'd tell me, 'You were the first person I met in Anchorage, my first friend!'"

A clipping dated April 6, 1946, from the *Times*, reported, "Welcome Hostess Greets 14 Recent Arrivals to City." It went on, "Mrs. Harrison, representing the city's merchants, calls on permanent families who establish homes in Anchorage. She carries gifts and merchandise coupons to them and explains the services offered by the town's businessmen who subscribe to her advertising plan. Mrs. Harrison reported that the fourteen families she visited varied from federal employees here on government contracts to people in private industry…. Mrs. Harrison feels that undoubtedly there were families moving into Anchorage in this inaugural month of the welcoming plan who were overlooked. She asks anyone who knows a permanent family resident establishing a new home here to report the new address to her so that she may make a welcoming call."

Lorene's own family moved during this time. In 1945, they moved across the street from their rented home on Sixth and I to a two-story apartment house and a three-bedroom apartment. Lorene remembers it as being "too small, constructed from scrap materials, with floors made from a bowling alley, the bathroom of poor quality, and a kitchen like a closet." Still, not being able to imagine a home without entertaining, Lorene saw to it that the home had many guests.

Lorene's mind never sits still. One idea leads to another, and it wasn't long before she settled on the concept for another new business venture. "I had always made my own hats, and hats for my friends. In those days in Anchorage, you had to order your hats by mail order catalogue. There was always the chance your neighbor would show up with the same hat!" She sold the Welcoming Service, and opened up a small millinery boutique, The Hat Box, on August 17, 1948.

Logo for Lorene's millinery boutique, The Hat Box, opened in 1948. "My entire stock - all 40 hats I had made - sold opening day."

She had worked for a month to make enough hats, all of her own stylish design, for the opening of her small shop. "It was at 429 G Street, and I paid $90 each month for rent," Lorene says. With her usual mettle, she had borrowed $1,750 from the bank and had taken out one ad in the *Times* for the opening of her business. "I was pioneering at that time, willing to take a chance," she states. "I sought to own my own business well before most women did. It was tough. Mr. George Mumford at National Bank of Alaska was a member of the Glee Club. He agreed to let me borrow the money to open my business. I wasn't smart enough to worry!"

Her estimate of "enough hats" — about 40 that she had ready for opening day — was quickly wiped out. "By 4 p.m. on that opening day, I didn't have a single hat left. One hat even sold for $40 – a great deal of money in those days!" Obviously, she was on to something, a business that would eventually last 30 years and move several times, and her original supply wasn't about to meet the demand. "You have to understand that these women, military wives who had been living Outside during the war, were very dressy. They wanted fashion shows and fine dress shops. We had the Betty Faris dress shop (where Artique is today), the Smart Shop at 4th and F, and Welches at Fourth and E."

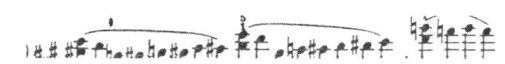

Quickly realizing that she wouldn't be able to make enough hats herself to satisfy her customers, Lorene wired a buyer Outside. "I gave her a little portrait of the community as a guide. Above all, I told her, there are no old people in Anchorage – at least no old people in spirit. So I don't want any 'old ladies' hats.'" With the opening of Lorene's Hat Box, gone were the days when hats were worn only for warmth in the town.

Buying trips and fashion shows associated with her Hat Box became some of Lorene's favorite activities over the years. "The hat shows were very popular," she says. "I did more than 250 shows in 30 years. There were big luncheons with hat shows once a month."

She even took The Hat Box to the radio. "I always did radio ads for my shop," Lorene recalls. "And I had a show called 'The Hat Box' through the 1950s on radio station KBYR. It was on every weekday morning at 7:30 a.m. for five minutes. I'd feature and talk about one hat per day."

It became a kind of traveling Hat Box, moving within the city. In 1953, Lorene was approached by Bob Atwood while she was standing in line at the bank. "You need more room," he told her, encouraging her to relocate to his building at

Lorene had her radio show, "The Hat Box," through the 1950s. "I'd feature and talk about one hat per day."

Fourth and E streets. "That was a big jump up for me," Lorene states. "My rent went up to $300 a month." Then in 1960, she moved the business to the Westward Hotel at Third and E streets, and doubled her

monthly rent to $600. "That was a very good location for The Hat Box," Lorene says. "There were lovely women's luncheons in the hotel, and after them, the women would flock to my shop. I loved it.

Bob Pond - Lorene calls him "the work horse" behind the early Anchorage Little Theatre, from which would spring many of the other arts organizations in Anchorage. She adds, "Bob is still giving wonderful plays and musicals, especially for children and the young crowd - now as director of Anchorage Community Theatre." In turn, Bob calls Lorene "the loveliest and most significant influence on the Anchorage arts in their entirety."

The best part of the business was always the people."

In 1972, Lorene moved The Hat Box once again, this time to a location on Fourth Avenue between E and F streets. "It was too huge," she admits. "The size took away from the intimacy I wanted." In 1972, she moved her business to the new University Center shopping mall. "I was one of the first businesses there." She called her shop simply "Lorene's" and expanded into a bridal and fine dress shop. She sold the business in December of 1978, at age 72, and 30 years after that first grand opening. Looking back over those three decades, Lorene summarizes, "I didn't make a fortune in money – but in friends."

Pioneering in the Arts

All through her years of business ownership, Lorene was triple timing, in a sense. She juggled her shop along with her family responsibilities, and took great steps to move the community ahead culturally. A group calling itself the Anchorage Little

Lorene conducts the chorus for "The Messiah" in 1947. The first community "Messiah" was performed in the high school auditorium on March 30 and 31 of that year. This performance has come to be known as the "first project of the Anchorage Community Chorus."

It's 1996 and the Anchorage Community Chorus is now known as the Concert Chorus. Grant Cochran, conductor, led the 165-voice chorus in its 50th anniversary performance.

Theatre was the catalyst for much that was to evolve in the young cultural community, and Lorene was named a charter member of its board of directors. Bob Pond, now director of Anchorage Community Theatre, looks back to the USO days for the seeds of what was to come.

"In 1944, the USO was a haven for the GI's. They wanted programs, and Lorene was there getting things going. Bruce Marcus, a GI who had been a professional actor in New York before joining the Army, was elected as director of a theater group at the USO. Their first production was 'Ladies in Retirement,' an old chestnut," Pond states. "Charlton Heston, then stationed at Fort Richardson, was approached to take a lead. When he said he was too busy to get involved, Frank Brink offered to direct the play — if Bruce Marcus would take the part."

The production was a success. "People began to say, 'We can do this,'" according to Pond. "Lorene and others got together and called themselves the Anchorage Little Theatre Group. They asked $3 for membership, and eventually had an official membership of 56 people around town. An Anchorage lawyer, J. Earl Cooper, helped them incorporate." The first production of the Anchorage Little Theatre Group was the play, *Our Town*, with A.B. See as its narrator. In December of 1946, the Little Theatre produced *A Christmas Carol*, under the direction of Frank Brink, with Lorene conducting a small chorus."

A few of the conductors from the early years of the chorus were honored at the 50th anniversary celebration. Here are Royal Norquist; Mary Hale; Lorene, founder of the Community Chorus; Wayne Baughman; and Calvin Rogers. Lorene comments, "We were there to congratulate the very splendid present conductor, Grant Cochran."

"Within two years," Bob Pond states, "the Anchorage Little Theatre seemed to begin everything. They helped to sponsor the first community *Messiah* at Easter of 1947 and looked at bringing up guest artists and starting a symphony. There were 13 members in the Little Theatre who could play something — some instrument. Ed De Paul got them together, and that group became the seeds of the symphony. By 1947, Charles Eroh took over conducting what was then called the nucleus of the *Messiah* choir. Lorene recalls, "The Presbyterian Church choir had decided in 1946 that it would be fun to do the *Messiah*, but to do it right it would take more than our 40-some voices. I wrote to the ministers of all the local churches, which by then included a Catholic, Episcopal, and a Lutheran church and the chapels on Fort Richardson, and invited

Maxim Schapiro (left) would become the founder of the Alaska Music Trail in 1950. Having fallen in love with Alaska when he came here as a performer sponsored by the Anchorage Little Theatre in 1947 and '48, he told Lorene, "I could get performers to come to Alaska 'to sing for their supper,'" The Anchorage Concert Association was formed that year, to sponsor the Anchorage portion of the Music Trail. Here, Mr. Schapiro is shown with Mel Peterson, ACA treasurer, and Lorene, president.

Anchorage Little Symphony."

The concept for a large choral performance of Handel's *Messiah* had come from the Presbyterian Church choir, and its 44 voices would form the

them to join in such a large community performance for the following Easter. Anchorage Little Theatre helped with the financing and the program. It seemed that they sponsored most everything in those days."

The event took place on Sunday afternoon and Monday evening, March 30 and 31 of 1947 with the program reading, "The Anchorage Little Theatre Presents a United Choir of All Faiths Assisted by the Anchorage Little Symphony." Lorene directed the combined choir of 98 vocalists with 22 instrumentalists accompanying, now known as the Anchorage Little Symphony. Seeds of the Community Chorus had been planted. In fact, four years later in a 1951 *Daily Times* newspaper article, this production of the *Messiah* was labeled "the Community Chorus' first project." The choir had raised money for the purchase of a Hammond organ, flown in for the performance, marking the first purchase of a Hammond organ in town.

Lorene meets Marita Farell, vocalist of the Metropolitan Opera, at the Anchorage International Airport with daughters, Pegge and Carol Anne. Marita would later live with the Harrisons while she assisted Lorene in the production of a show called "the Arctic Summeretta" and moved toward the founding of the Anchorage Opera.

Lorene looks back in her own words to this great flurry of cultural activity in the mid-1940s. "I was on the board of directors of the Anchorage Little Theatre then, whose main purpose was to produce plays. They made some money doing that, so later sponsored the Little Symphony Orchestra, the Community Chorus, and in 1946, appointed me as chairman of a committee — with Anne Dimond and Hal Bockoven on the committee — to investigate bringing an 'Outside' artist to Anchorage. (We three had brought this idea to the board's attention.) Grant Johannesen, pianist, was selected as a kind of 'test case,' and was brought north from Salt Lake City for a March 28th concert in 1947. He had been recommended by a writer at the *Times*, Ruthella Wade. That concert sold out the high school auditorium, and was so highly successful that people were saying, 'We need more!'

"In October we brought up another pianist, Maxim Schapiro, world-recognized performer. He was originally from Russia, but came to Anchorage from New York. His was another very successful concert. Maxim had a great sense of humor. An earthquake occurred during his performance. He just slid his stool closer to the piano, and kept on playing! He was so impressed with Alaska and with the music community here. He loved Alaska. He saw here a community of 'doers, not just viewers,' and wanted to become a part of it. We had him come back in 1948, and also brought in a vocal duo, Marita Farell and Lansing Hatfield, from the Met."

Here Lorene pauses to tell one of her many personal stories about the musicians performing in Anchorage and so often entertained in her home. "Marita and Lansing had performed in Fairbanks before coming to Anchorage for their concert. I met them at the airport, along with their pianist, and on Thanksgiving Day, Jack brought them over from the hotel for dinner at our home at 619 I Street. It was small and cramped, and I had to move the kitchen table into the living room and expand it to seat everyone. I had out my sterling and fine china and glassware. Lansing was a big man who loved to drink, and he bumped into the table. I could see things flying! Jack had to put him to bed upstairs. I could tell that Marita was so embarrassed. The concert was that evening, and by intermission, Lansing was asked not to continue singing — he had been leaning against the piano as if to fall,

October 10, 1950 - the newly formed Anchorage Concert Association presents its first concert - violinist Roman Totenberg (on the left). Here he is congratulated after his perfomance by Lorene, founder and the first president of the Concert Association, and Maxim Schapiro, pianist and founder of the Alaska Music Trail.

and a board member had asked him to leave. Marita would have to do the second half of the concert by herself. She ran the two blocks to my home during the intermission, picked over my solo music, and returned in time for the second half!"

Lorene continues with her story of the part Maxim Schapiro would play in Alaska's music scene. "In October 1949, Maxim Schapiro was back again to accompany cellist, Luigi

Silva. By 1950, he conceived the idea of bringing some of his many artist friends from around the world north to Alaska's four largest towns – Anchorage, Juneau, Fairbanks, and Ketchikan. He would call his project, his dream, the Alaska Music Trail." (Lorene adds that by this time, the Anchorage Little Theatre had decided not to bring in guest artists, and to concentrate on the production of plays.) She explains, "Maxim would bring the artists north, but each of the four communities would have to have its own organization to handle their local arrangements for the artists, and bringing music to the children in the schools in these towns was of utmost importance to him as well."

Lorene continues, "At that time I called together the presidents of 16 local service and social groups to meet and organize the Anchorage part of the Music Trail. After several preliminary meetings, the group met officially on July 20, 1950 in the studios of KENI Radio and drafted the constitution and bylaws for what was to be known as the Anchorage Concert Association." The meeting was reported the next day in the *Times*, July 21, 1950. "Concert Association Sponsors Fall Series," the headline reads, and then the following is reported. "Mrs. Jack Harrison was unanimously elected president of the Anchorage Concert Association, formally organized at a meeting in the KENI studios last night. The organization was formed by 16 representatives of

Dr. Robert Wilkins and Lorene join hands, many years after they first worked together in the mid 1950s on the board of the Anchorage Concert Association. Dr. Wilkins became managing director of the association, a volunteer position, in 1957. Lorene comments, "Without him on board, I now wonder how we would have managed." Dr. Wilkins is very involved in the association to this day.

local groups, to continue the annual concert series formerly sponsored by the Anchorage Little Theatre. The name was chosen from several suggested....

"Organizations and their representatives included Paul Warber, Anchorage Chamber of Commerce; George Jackson, Junior Chamber of Commerce; Keith Lesh, Rotary Club; Willard Thomas, Kiwanis; Earl Cooper, Lions.

"Mrs. C.O. Brown, Anchorage Woman's Club; Mrs. James Hurst, Soroptimist; Mrs. Gladys Grady, Business and Professional Women; Mrs. Jack Faulds, Officers' Wives Club.

"Mrs. Irene Cleaves, NCO Wives Club; Mrs. R.L. Chamberlain, Beta Sigma Phi; Mrs. Jack Harrison, Anchorage Little Theatre; Mel Peterson, Parent Teachers Association.

"Peter Britch, Anchorage Symphony; Lt. Russell Mason, Anchorage Community Chorus; Opal Lu Smith, *Anchorage News*....

"Plans call for concert artists to be obtained for an Alaska circuit covering nine or more cities. Those which have already indicated acceptance of

In 1981, Ira Perman was hired as the executive director of the Anchorage Concert Association, the first full time paid position, and one he still holds. He had been a volunteer with the association before he was hired, and is shown here with one of the Paratore Brothers (back to the camera), duo pianists who performed in Anchorage in 1979. (They returned in 1998.) Lorene calls his hiring "the smartest thing the association ever did," and adds, "Ira has been at the helm to make the ACA an annual million-dollar business."

the planned series are Anchorage, Juneau, Ketchikan, Fairbanks, Cordova, Seward, Sitka, Wrangell, and Petersburg. Several other cities including Palmer and Kodiak have indicated an interest in the plan."

Lorene served as president of the

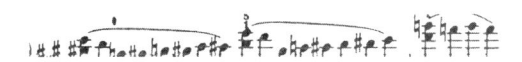

board of directors for the first two years of the association. "The third year, I declined the nomination, saying, 'This is a community project, not a Harrison organization.' However, the group recommended that I remain on the board permanently as vice president, which I did until 1957." (She would again serve as president of the board in 1964 and 1975, its silver anniversary year.)

She continues, "It was then in the mid-1950s that Dr. Bob Wilkins came into the picture. He was greatly interested, with experience from 'Outside.'" Looking back, Lorene continues, "Without him on board, I now wonder how we would have managed. He was wonderful at finding many of the performers." To this day, Lorene feels that there have continued to be "a few enthusiasts from the very early days of the Concert Association, and very many new residents interested and supportive." She adds, "The smartest thing that happened was when Ira Perman was made executive director in 1981. He'd been a volunteer with the association for two years prior to that. There are now enough dedicated members and volunteers to carry on well into this next century. What a powerful arts organization is ours — the Anchorage Concert Association! I'm very, very proud to have founded it!"

Lorene continues, "Through all these early years of the Concert Association, I never got paid for what I did. I just loved doing the work and seeing the results. My pay was in the experience and the fun. I can remember the first dollar I received for this work. It was in 1971. I'd been entertaining so many of the artists — cooking for them at home or taking them out to eat, meeting their planes and driving them wherever they needed to go, having them for extended stays in my home. Richard Anglemyer was treasurer of the Concert Association then. 'Here,' he said to me. 'Here's a hundred dollars to take performers out to eat.' That was the first time I'd been paid."

While the organization of the Anchorage Concert Association was going on, Maxim Schapiro continued to plan out his Music Trail, a trail that would eventually be comprised of 17 cities and towns as subscribers, in Alaska and western Canada. The four larger towns would have all the performers come to them in concert, while the smaller towns would receive artists selected for them by Maxim. "How lucky we were that Maxim fell in love with Alaska, and we became his chosen people!" Lorene declares. His enthusiasm for Alaska brimming over, he'd tell Lorene, "I have friends who would come to this Territory to perform, just for their supper!"

Lorene explains how his Music Trail operated. "Each of these communities paid Maxim as subscribers to organize the schedule and transportation to their locations. Maxim received $2500 a year to act as an agent for the artists. Communities then handled their own local arrangements. I worked as a volunteer in Anchorage, handling the details here."

An article in the *Seattle Times*, dated January 30, 1952, describes the logistics and plotting out of the Music Trail. "Alaska – the last frontier – has opened a new lane. The Alaska Trail of Music (sic.) has been formed by housewives and businessmen to bring 'outside' musical artists to a dozen Alaska towns, according to Mrs. Jack Harrison of Anchorage. Mrs. Harrison should know, for she spurred her city's Little Theater (sic.) into sponsoring its first concert by an outside artist, Grant Johannesen, pianist….Mr. Johannesen played in Anchorage in 1947 and also in Fairbanks, Juneau, and Ketchikan. From 1947 – 49, the Little Theater sponsored such performers as Kenneth Spencer, Marita Farell, Carol Brice, and Maxim Schapiro. In 1949 the theater group relinquished its backing and it fell to Mrs. Harrison to continue the concerts (in Anchorage)….With the aid of Mr. Schapiro, Mrs. Harrison started the Alaska Trail." (Lorene would be the first to clarify this point. "Maxim started the Music Trail," she states. "It was his dream. I was just one-seventeenth of the overall project, organizing Anchorage, one of the 17 communities on the Trail.") The *Seattle Times* article continues, "The performers are handpicked according to ability and how they will adapt themselves to Alaska ways….The circuit is no joy ride for the performers." (Remember, this is being written out of Seattle.) "Rugged Alaska is still rugged and poor flying weather and unfinished roads would disturb the temperament of most any artist. The show hits the road in Cordova, and plays Seward, Kodiak, Anchorage, Fairbanks, Juneau, Sitka, Petersburg, Wrangell, Ketchikan, Metlakatla, and Prince Rupert, all within three weeks. The accommodations include high school auditoriums, gymnasiums, church halls, and frequently misused school pianos. The performers soon overlook the simple arrangements and warm to the wholehearted response of the audiences. The towns have formed separate music associations and most are saving funds to purchase better equipment. Three concerts are given each season, with hopes for four next year."

A kind of follow-up story appeared two days later, this time in the *Seattle Post-Intelligencer*, on February 1, 1952. Under the heading "Anchorage Musician Visits Here," the article reported, "If you think Anchorage, Alaska is the jumping-off place, think again! We just talked with Mrs. Jack Harrison of that co-old northern metropolis, and now we'd never think of traveling Arctic-ward without our best bejeweled cocktail hat and our dancing shoes. No cultural icebowl, either, Anchorage has an up-and-coming Concert Association, which Mrs. Harrison heads for the third year, in addition to managing her millinery business, The Hat Box, and such extracurricular assignments as Anchorage's official hostess, leader of the Presbyterian Church choir and former director of the Anchorage Community Chorus.

"Mrs. Harrison's Seattle visit (which mixed business with pleasure) took on an added aura of excitement this week when she chatted with conductor Arthur Fiedler and Mrs. Ruth McCreery, manager of the Seattle Symphony, regarding a possible Alaska tour of the 75-musician group. Still strictly in the dream stage, the tour cannot be scheduled until the Anchorage impresarios overcome such obstacles as lack of an auditorium sufficiently large for an appearance and housing for 75 visitors in an already swollen boom town of between 30,000 and 40,000 residents."

The article goes on to explain, "Transportation from concert to concert is usually by air, but is sometimes uncertain and uncomfortable. Soprano Tomiko Kanazawa and Cesare Curzi, San Francisco tenor, recently joggled from Anchorage to Seward via taxicab over an unfinished road to meet a concert curtain-time when their plane was grounded." Lorene adds to this story. "Oh, I remember Tomiko's visit so well. On top of the travel hazards, her concert dress was stolen from the Seward Methodist Church while she was having dinner after her performance. When she got back to Anchorage, she quickly went over to Mrs. Dodi Walkowski's store and bought a new one."

Lorene returns to the fact that bringing music to the school children was of great importance to Maxim Schapiro on the Music Trail. "The contract that each town signed as a subscriber to the

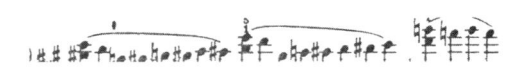

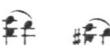

Alaska Music Trail actually included the requirement that the artists give performances in the schools," Lorene explains. "And Maxim insisted that the children pay something for these performances, to involve them and foster the concept of the value of the music in the children. He did not believe that they should be free."

Maxim continued to lead the Music Trail with great enthusiasm until his sudden death in the fall of 1958. His widow, Jane (later Mrs. Martin Livingston) would carry on with the productions, with the support of Martin, until the couple retired in 1970.

In 1950, Lorene made her first buying trip Outside to New York City for The Hat Box. Wearing more than one hat herself, she would eventually combine hat-buying with scouting for potential performers for the Anchorage concerts. "It became a pattern for Maxim to go to New York ahead of me, and line up suggestions of performers for me to hear while I was in the city on buying trips," Lorene explains. "These trips were wonderful – just wonderful – concerts, operas, and Broadway shows combined with dinners in many delightful little places in the city." Through a contact made during the war years, Lorene was provided with "beautiful quarters" in the Waldorf Astoria Hotel on these New York trips. "Art Johnson was an opera hound, here in the military, who had sung in the Presbyterian Church Choir during the 1940s," she explains. "Sometimes we entertain angels unaware. He would come over to my home and listen to my collection of recordings. After the war, he went to New York City and became the credit manager at the Waldorf. He had told me that if I ever got to the city, to contact him and he'd see that I got a beautiful room at a reduced price. For 20 years of buying trips, he did just that for me."

In 1949, Lorene put together another production called the Arctic Summeretta, presented by the Anchorage Little Theatre. She directed and Frank Brink staged this new musical extravaganza on June 20, 21, and 22 in the high school auditorium to sold-out audiences. "We'd held a contest to name this new show. It was not an opera; it was not an operetta; but it was held in the summer. The name Summeretta was chosen," Lorene states. Marita Farell was a lead vocalist, and many of the songs presented were from the musical, *Oklahoma*. Simeon Oliver's arrangement of *Aleut Lullaby* was also featured.

Marita met Lorene in New York City on her buying trip in 1950, and the two attended the Broadway production of *South Pacific*. After a one-year hiatus, they brought back the Summeretta, this time featuring many of the songs from *South Pacific*. Marita came back to Anchorage from New York City and lived with the Harrisons for several months to prepare this second Summeretta. Lorene wrote the original story line to tie the production together. A glowing review of this second Summeretta in the *Anchorage Daily News* (June 20, 1951), called it "delightful and artistic entertainment" playing to a full auditorium for four nights. There was a combined chorus and symphony, and Marita was once again the leading vocalist. Like Maxim Schapiro, she had bonded with Alaska, and would put down roots for the musical community. Lorene comments, "Marita grew to like it here so much, she moved here with her husband and lived here for seven years. She even started our first opera company — the Anchorage Civic Opera, in 1961. It was formally incorporated in 1962."

Wouldn't you know — Lorene was on the founding board of directors. A program for the Anchorage Opera's production of *Pirates of Penzance* in the fall of 1997 traced the history of the opera back to these Summeretta performances in 1949 and 1951, clarifying the point that the roots for opera in Anchorage go back well beyond 1962. This history states, "Credit for starting an opera company in Anchorage goes to Lorene Harrison as does credit for initiating most of the community's musical organizations."

A little "short story" follows in the program. "Evangeline Atwood said, 'Lorene says we should have an opera company, so I guess we'll have to make one.' And so they did." The first season, 1961 – 62, included *Die Fledermaus*, *The Vagabond King*, and *Hansel and Gretel*. Opera was off and running in Anchorage, although there were some floundering years for the opera company in the mid-60s, following Marita's return to New York City.

In her own outlines of the history of the musical arts in Anchorage, Lorene lists Marita Farell as the opera's founder. She mentions Doc Purnell, the manager of KBYR and an opera lover, as the first president of the board with Evangeline Atwood and Bob Wilkins also serving on the original board of directors.

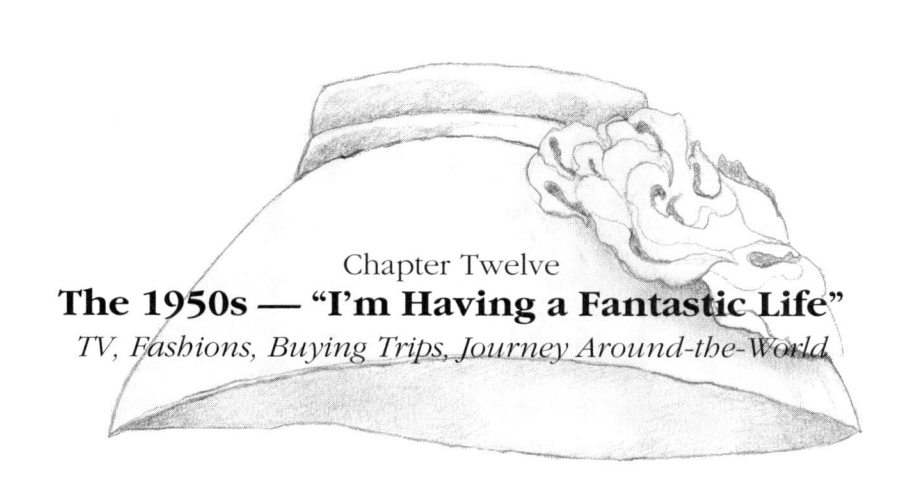

Chapter Twelve
The 1950s — "I'm Having a Fantastic Life"
TV, Fashions, Buying Trips, Journey Around-the-World

With this great flurry of activity in the 1940s and '50s, contributing so much of note to the cultural and fashion scenes in Anchorage, it is not surprising that Lorene Harrison was named "First Lady of Anchorage" in 1951. Telling of this recognition, the *Daily Times* reported on March 17, 1951, "Anchorage's 'First Lady' has been first in musical and theatrical circles in Anchorage for the past 17 years. Mrs. Jack Harrison has been selected by representatives of 16 local civic clubs as their choice for their honor. Although the 'woman of the year' contest has been sponsored nationally in the states for the past several years, this is the first time a selection has been made in Anchorage. The contest is sponsored by Beta Sigma Phi sorority, and in addition to the award presented to Mrs. Harrison, carries with it an honorary membership in the organization." (Lorene had been the first sponsor of a chapter of Beta Sigma Phi in Alaska, back in 1942.) Jeanne Laurence made the official presentation of the award at the Elks Hall, setting for the sorority's Easter fashion show.

This was just the beginning of many accolades coming her way in the 1950s. In October of 1953, the *Daily Times* made much of a dinner held at the First Presbyterian Church to honor Lorene, leaving her position as choir director there. The paper

Mostly Music

1951 – a Beta Sigma Phi tea held in the Elks Hall to honor Lorene as "the First Lady of Anchorage." With her are (left to right) Mabel Vaara, Jeanne Laurence, and Marjorie Learned.

Beta Sigma Phi has long been important to Lorene. Shown here, posed on the steps in the Anchorage Hotel, is the first Anchorage chapter, organized in 1944. The organizer, from Kansas City headquarters, is in the front row, third from the left. Lorene is also in the front row, second from the right. Next to her, in the dark dress, Jeanne Laurence is seated. (Both Jeanne and her husband Sydney had their artists' studios in the Anchorage Hotel.) Lorene was an International Honorary Member of Beta Sigma Phi in 1956. She adds, "There are now 13 chapters in Anchorage."

stated, "Mrs. Jack Harrison is to be honored at a church family dinner tonight at First Presbyterian Church in appreciation of her 19 years of service as choir director. She has asked for a leave of absence due to the press of other activities." It would prove to be just that – a leave of absence – and Lorene would return to directing the choir in the 1960s.

On the home front, some of that "press of activities" had revolved around the recent move of the family home to a two-story, split-level house at Tenth and N streets on the Park Strip –- 1242 West 10th Avenue. She and Jack purchased this home in 1952. Later, in 1965, Lorene added on a third-floor addition ("the better to entertain you with"). This was her home for 30 years, from 1952 to 1982, and provided an inviting, warm home-away-from-home for many visiting guest musicians. Bob Atwood in the *Anchorage Times,* called it "the hospitality house for visiting dignitaries."

A local reporter described it as follows: "Mrs. Harrison lives in a tastefully furnished house on Tenth Street with a beige dog named Emily and a fine view of the Susitna mountains. Here she has a workroom crammed with papers, envelopes, and business correspondence which, though orderly, is more rococo than office-functional. And she has her 'music room' with phonograph and records and comfortable furniture and a wall gallery of artists' photographs inscribed to

Still active in Beta Sigma Phi, Lorene is shown here officiating at a chapter ceremony in November, 1990. "I love these girls," Lorene says of her sorority sisters.

herself." (*Anchorage Daily News*, January 26, 1963)

Today, she still has her collection of photos, displayed on several tall, fold-back screens in her room

The Harrison family home, at the corner of 10th and N (1242 West 10th), in 1952 when Lorene and Jack bought it.

The Harrison home in 1964 with recent improvements.

The home in 1965, with the addition of the third floor, for entertaining guests.

This is the home in 1982, when Lorene sold it.

in the Anchorage Pioneers' Home. There are photos of such world-famous artists as Leonard Bernstein, Eugene Ormandy, Van Cliburn, Marilyn Horne, Fred Waring, and Isaac Stern. Many of the artists pictured in the collection have become her lifelong friends. "Van Cliburn is one of my dearest friends," Lorene relates, while showing his autographed photo. "His mother became very excited about The Hat Box. She bought four hats in my store, and told me there was no store in New York where she could ever find four hats she would want to buy!"

Van Cliburn's sentiments speak for the many gathered over the years by Lorene and her "hospitality house." In gratitude for Lorene's friendship, he wrote on his photo, "For Lorene – With remembrance of our wonderful visit with you as well as all your kind thoughts and superb hospitality. Your charming personality and graciousness naturally assure you an indelible place in the hearts of so many people. Our warmest wishes and deepest appreciation. Sincerely ever, Van Cliburn, 9 May, 1966."

One year later, in a letter dated May 23, 1967, Lorene received the following personal letter from Eugene Ormandy.

Lorene's Gallery — Her collection of photos, frequently personally autographed, from guest performers who so often became life-long friends - This photo of Lorene and her Gallery was taken in 1978.

Mostly Music

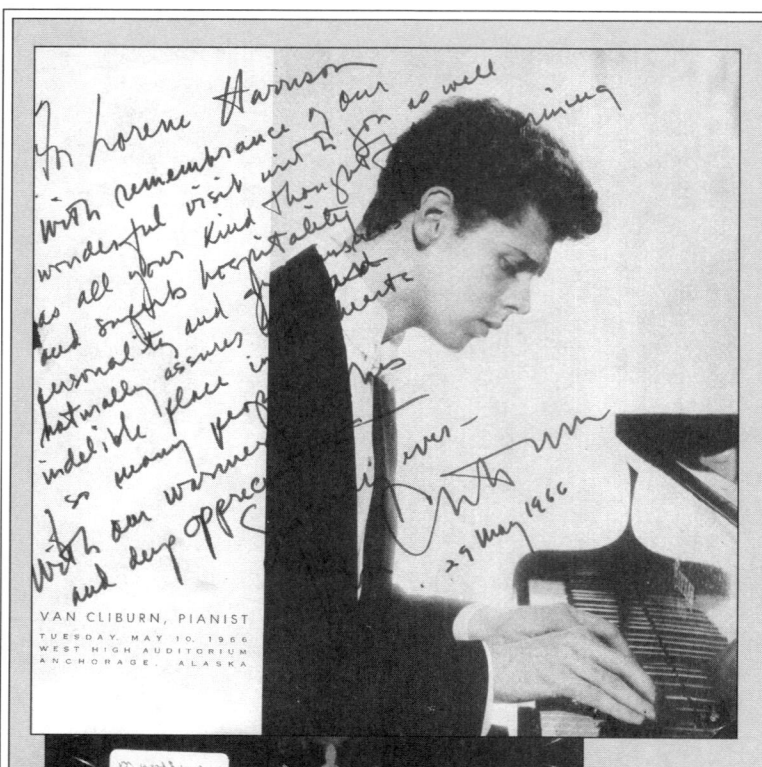

Van Cliburn - "To Lorene Harrison with remembrances of our wonderful visit with you as well as all your kind thoughts and superb hospitality. Your charming personality and graciousness naturally assures you an indelible place in the hearts of so many people - With our warmest and deep appreciation - Sincerely ever, Van Cliburn, 29 May 1966" - Lorene remembers that he came to Anchorage with his mother and father.

VAN CLIBURN, PIANIST
TUESDAY, MAY 10, 1966
WEST HIGH AUDITORIUM
ANCHORAGE, ALASKA

Marilyn Horne - "To Lorene ! - Thank you so much for all your kindnesses. I look forward to our continued friendship in the coming years - Fondest best wishes, Marilyn Horne, 1959."

Leonard Bernstein — 1961. Lorene remembers a telegram. "He sent it after the 1964 earthquake wondering if there was something he could do to help."

The Romeros - *Father, and 3 sons - Celin, Pepe and Angel. (Again Lorene shares a favorite story. "In September of 1966, I was picking up all four Romeros at the airport. Each one had his expensive guitar tucked between his legs in my car - when the car caught fire! Smoke everywhere! I never saw four men move so quickly. They each grabbed their guitars, sprang out of my car, and ran!" The story ends well. Dr. Wilkins was driving right behind her, and took the Romeros and their rescued guitars on to the hotel.")*

Lucine Amara *from the Metroplitan Opera- "To Lorene ! - It is wonderful to know you - Sincerely, Lucine, 1953." (Lorene shares a favorite story about taking Lucine potato picking when she was preparing one of her home-cooked dinners for this guest artist. "She loved potato picking! She even brought a sack along, filled it with potatoes, and threw it over her shoulder.")*

The Romero family *in California at Celin's home, where Lorene had dinner with them all and the children.*

Mostly Music

Dear Mrs. Harrison:

Words cannot express our gratitude for all you did for us while we were in Anchorage. I believe I speak for all my colleagues in the orchestra when I say that we have never experienced warmer hospitality anywhere in our travels, and special thanks to you for taking such good care of us.

Eugene Ormandy - *"To Lorene Harrison - The inspiration in the musical city of Anchorage - with all good wishes - Eugene Ormandy, May 22, 1967."*

We will not forget you and your wonderful personality and we hope some day we may pay you a return visit, or perhaps we may have the great pleasure of having you visit us in our home territory so that we may reciprocate in some way for your many kindnesses.

A picture is on its way for your 'gallery,' ….

With warmest good wishes always, in which my wife joins me, I am
Most cordially yours,
Eugene Ormandy

Lorene speaks with great admiration about Eugene Ormandy, telling a story she sees as character revealing. "The day after his performance, I was taking Eugene and his wife to the airport. Sadly, just the night before, Concert Association board member John Collins had had a heart attack, climbing all those many steps at West High, to get to the auditorium. He had been rushed to the hospital. I told Eugene about this as I was driving. He thought for a moment. Then he asked, 'How much would a nice bouquet of flowers cost?' I told him about $35. He got out his wallet and handed me the $35. Then he wrote on a card, 'Hoping for a quick recovery.' Unfortunately John died that day, but the flowers and the gesture meant so much to his family. I believe Eugene Ormandy showed his true colors that day — that beyond his musical interests he was a true humanitarian."

In addition to the move in the 1950s, other landmark family events in that decade had been the marriage of daughter Pegge to Joseph Vielbig in 1953. This was followed by the marriage of daughter Carol Anne to Robert Dodd in 1956.

A landmark event in the history of musical arts in Anchorage occurred in 1954. Lorene labels it a "great set-back." "That year the high school auditorium burned to the ground. It had served as the Anchorage Municipal Auditorium. We lost not only the performance space, but also a Steinway grand piano and other instruments, along with risers and platforms. Performances moved to the Empress Theater and the Elks Hall. The auditorium was rebuilt in 1955 and dedicated as the Sydney Laurence Auditorium. And we were all relieved when the West High School Auditorium was completed, with its 2,000 seats, in 1956."

On a brighter personal note, in 1954, the same year as the fire,

Lorene met Raja and Shala, who danced in a style from India, when they were here for an Anchorage concert performance in 1969. They autographed a photo to her: "Dear Mrs. Harrison; It has been an experience-and-a-half meeting and knowing you. Here's hoping this is the beginning of a long friendship. Most sincerely. Shala and Raja." Predictably, some 30 years later, Lorene is still in touch with them. "Shala and I always remember each others' birthdays, and stay in touch each Christmas," Lorene says.

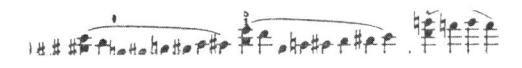

Lorene was selected by the Anchorage Women's Club as its nominee

for Alaska Territorial Mother of the Year, an annual contest sponsored nationally by the Golden Rule Foundation. Stacks of letters came to this foundation, in support of Lorene's nomination. In reporting this honor, an article in the Anchorage newspapers catches us up on these activities of Lorene and her family by this time. "Mrs. Harrison is well known for her civic and social activities and is owner-manager of The Hat Box….She is a member of the Soroptimist Club, serves on the civic affairs committee of the Chamber of Commerce, was first sponsor of Beta Sigma Phi in Alaska, is an honorary life member of the Anchorage Little Theatre, an honorary life member of the Anchorage Community Chorus which she organized in 1946, and member of the Anchorage Concert Association which she organized and served as first president.

"Although devoting so much of her time to civic projects, Mrs. Harrison has maintained a real home for her husband and daughters. Pegge Lee Vielbig, after making a fine scholastic record in the Anchorage public schools,

Daughter Pegge's wedding to Joe Vielbig at First Presbyterian Church, 1953— The wedding party, left to right: Diane Kroesing, Donna Killeen, Marilyn Haines, Carol Anne Harrison, Pegge, Joe Vielbig, Klindt Vielbig (Joe's twin brother), Gordon Stang, Bill Wyatt, and Russ Lamoreaux.

The bride and groom, Pegge and Joe, at their wedding reception.

Carol Anne and Bob's reception - with Ruth Dodd "pouring" at the end of the reception table, then Gladys Swank, Gerry Kirchner, Marita Farell dipping punch for Carl Morton, George Mumford, and Nell Mary Morton talking to Ruth.

The bride and groom, Carol Anne and Bob, at their wedding reception.

Daughter Carol Anne's wedding to Bob Dodd at First Presbyterian Church, 1956.

graduated last year from Whitman College in Walla Walla, Wash. with a Bachelor of Science degree. Her husband will receive his master's degree from Stanford graduate school this year.

"Carol Anne Harrison is well known locally as one of the princesses in the 1954 Fur Rendezvous Queen's

Jack and Lorene at their 25th wedding anniversary, July 3, 1955 - "We had a small party at our home."

court. Her interests are in the field of dramatics, journalism, singing, and skating. She is a graduate of local schools and has completed one year of college." Like her sister, she had been attending Whitman.

At this time, husband Jack was vice president of Anchorage Sand and Gravel, following his career as a locomotive engineer for the Alaska Railroad, and ownership of the Cinder Concrete Products Company. He'd been active on the board of trustees of the First Presbyterian Church and the Chamber of Commerce, and was involved in volunteer work for the Boy Scouts. In 1957, Jack and Lorene built a log cabin — "three rooms and a path" – as she describes it, on five acres at Mile 102 on the Old Glenn Highway, overlooking the Matanuska Glacier. Lorene grew to love this spot. Minus running water and electricity, it became a kind of rugged Alaska hospitality house, another place to entertain friends.

As if all this activity were not enough, Lorene had decided to shine her talents in a new direction in 1954. She began a woman's television show. It would be another in the line of her pioneering ventures. "I'd never even seen a woman's television show. What would happen on such a show?" Lorene remembers asking herself. Television was relatively new in the city — only about a year old, she thinks — and there was one station, KFIA (K-First in Alaska), on channel 2, affiliated with both ABC and CBS.

Her live show was called "Lorene's Scrapbook," and Lorene recalls how this new venture came about.

Lorene Harrison

The cabin path (below), bordered by wildflowers.

The cabin (above) that Jack and Lorene built in 1957 at Mile 102 of the Glenn Highway, overlooking the Matanuska Glacier - "Oh, how I loved that place!" Here, family pet, Emily, follows Lorene to the cabin. "All the landscaping was yet to be done when Jack took this photo," Lorene comments. "There is a door at my right with bedroom to the left on the lower level, a stairway going directly up from the doorway to the 'everything' room. It was heated with a kerosene stove, with the oven for both heat and cooking."

The carport under the glassed-in porch - "The view was terrific," Lorene states.

Mostly Music

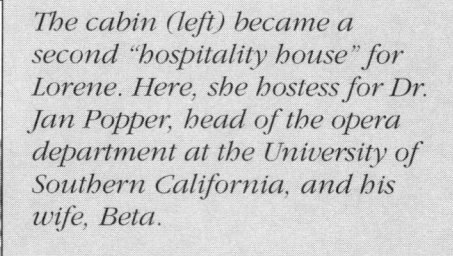

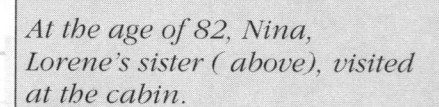

The cabin (left) became a second "hospitality house" for Lorene. Here, she hostess for Dr. Jan Popper, head of the opera department at the University of Southern California, and his wife, Beta.

At the age of 82, Nina, Lorene's sister (above), visited at the cabin.

Lorene (left) shares a later photo of Dr. Jan Popper, here with Natalie Limonick. "They both stayed at my house during operas over the years. Natalie was Dr. Popper's accompanist, and 'next-in-line' to head the opera department at USC. They and Jan's wife, Beta, were all very special!"

"I'd been doing ads for The Hat Box for the TV station, once a week, for about 15 minutes. I was the commentator, featuring my hats. A shoe company and Carol's Dress Shop were also included, and I lined up all the models. Really, I suppose we were doing the first infomercials!" She'd been spotted by Bard Melton, the station manager. "He came into my store one day, and just burst out with his idea. He told me, 'We want to start a woman's television show. We got together a list of names of women who could do the show — and we keep coming back to one name. It's yours!' I was surprised, to say the least. He went on to explain what would be involved. 'You'd have to get all your own sponsors. You'd be live on the air, and we'd want you to do some cooking, some sewing, some entertaining and conversing, some listing of community events — anything you think women would be interested in.'"

All this gave even Lorene and her boundless energy reason to pause. "I was stunned," Lorene states simply. "And he wanted the show to be on every weekday, for 45 minutes, but soon to be a full hour!" On top of everything else, Lorene remembers

"An informative and entertaining program designed especially for the ladies....." - "Lorene's Scrapbook" went on the air on Channel 2 in 1954, then KENI-TV. This was the logo for Lorene's live, one-hour show, every weekday. According to Lorene, TV had come to Anchorage only about one year earlier - in 1953.

that this proposal came just minutes after Louise Brown, then president of the Anchorage Women's Club, had come into her shop to tell her that the club was nominating her for the Mother of the Year award. "She'd just gone out the door when in came Bard," Lorene laughs.

History tells us that Lorene said "yes," and went on the air. "I don't know how I did it," she admits. A half-page ad appeared, complete with Lorene's smiling photo, looking composed and confident, in the *Anchorage Times*, June 7, 1954.

"Starting Tuesday, June 8th on Channel 2, 4:00 – 5:00 p.m. — 'Lorene's Scrapbook' – AN INFORMATIVE AND ENTERTAINING PROGRAM DESIGNED ESPECIALLY FOR THE LADIES . . . . FEATURING ANCHORAGE'S OWN LORENE HARRISON! – YOU WON'T WANT TO MISS ONE SINGLE PAGE OF 'LORENE'S SCRAPBOOK.'

Every Tuesday, Wednesday and Thursday ON CHANNEL 2, KFIA-TV, Anchorage – ABC & CBS AFFILIATE"

Lorene remembers trying to measure up to this bold proclamation, scrambling to get ready for her first show. "I grabbed some of my favorite recipes and lined up some advertisers and some guests to interview. You must remember that this was live TV — no going back." She decided to open each show singing and playing the piano. "***You'll find your happiness lies, right under your eyes, back in your own backyard.***" That became her theme song, letting the women of Anchorage know that they were about to be entertained and informed — not without some on-air foibles.

Lorene admits there was a lot to learn. "A city election was coming up, and a lady, a Democrat, approached me, asking if she could come on the show. I said, 'Sure, I'd be delighted.' Well, you can imagine that the Republicans came after me. 'How come you invited her?' I hadn't expected that at the time."

Then there was a cameraman and a newscaster who took pleasure in trying to make Lorene laugh on the air. "They were buddies — out to get me. I remember one day the newscaster brought in this little rubber doll and he kept flapping it at me on the side. I lost it for awhile."

In addition to lining up the advertisers, Lorene had to gather props to represent what was being sold. "It was on a Friday," Lorene recalls. "I was doing an ad for Anchorage Grocery Store, and I had my visuals for their weekend specials piled up on a table. 'Here are three cans of peas for such-and-such a price,' I said, holding them up. 'And here is a bunch of bananas offered at a bargain price.' I showed them. 'And here are two rolls of toilet tissue at this special price, two for one —

Lorene Harrison

Lorene opened her TV program each day, playing the piano, and singing her theme song - "You'll find your happiness lies, Right under your eyes, Back in your own backyard."

Getting ready for her show, "Lorene's Scrapbook" - "I'd cook in my kitchen at home, starting the 'finished project' for the live TV show."

Live on the air, from 1954-1958, Lorene would whip up some of her favorite recipes…

… and put them on the stove in the Channel 2 kitchen-set to simmer.

offered just for your weekend.' I should have known that those two buddies would interpret this to mean 'just for your weak end.' So much for their composure – and mine."

The show did well, despite inevitable live-broadcast glitches, and was on the air for four years. Like so many of Lorene's endeavors, it would be an award winner. A newspaper article, dated May 2, 1955, reports, "People from as far away as Washington, D.C., and Seattle were present Saturday night to receive awards for distinguished service to Alaska at the third annual Alaska Press Club award dinner in the Forest Park Country Club." The dinner recognized leadership in territorial affairs and presented awards of merit in journalism, radio and TV. Lorene was one of 15 honored that night, receiving an award for her women's TV show, along with Z.J. Loussac, given a citation for "his gift of the new public library, the largest gift given in the territory."

A national television appearance lay ahead. Lorene had met Arlene Francis, star of an NBC program called "Home Show" at a convention of the American Women in Radio and Television in New York in 1955.

As a member of American Women in Radio and TV, Lorene attended a convention in New York in the mid 50s. "The 'New York Times' asked for a photo of me as I was getting off the plane, since I was recognized as the newest member of the professional organization, and the member who had traveled the farthest to the meeting. This is that photo. At the convention I sat at the same table as Jackie Kennedy. Her husband, John F. Kennedy, was campaigning for president at the time, and was a convention speaker."

An article in the *Anchorage Times*, January 8, 1957, relates what happened next. "At the time Miss Francis expressed great interest in Alaska. Since then she and Mrs. Harrison have corresponded with the view of some time having an Alaska program." When Lorene was invited to appear two years later, she was excited. It would be an opportunity for her to wave Alaska's flag for statehood. "It was quite an experience being on the NBC national network for 30 minutes, sharing pride in Alaska," Lorene says. Husband Jack and daughter Carol Anne, then a flight attendant for Alaska Airlines, appeared with her. The family's enthusiasm for Alaska caught on nationally, and Lorene remembers that "the Chamber received bags of mail and I had to get the help of a secretary to answer my individual mail."

Broadening her scope from New York City to a trip around-the-world was all part of what led Lorene to declare in a newspaper interview, "I am having a fascinating life" — just one year after this national TV appearance. It was 1958 when Brad Phillips, owner of the first and only Anchorage travel agency at the time, asked Lorene if she and Jack would like to be part of the 63-day world tour he was organizing. "I'd always been interested in travel, in seeing how other people in other places do things," Lorene states. "Of course I said yes. Brad had been interested in having me as a partner in his travel business, and this trip would, in a sense, let me see what I'd be selling if I joined him as a business partner."

Back in 1951, during the Korean War, Lorene had satisfied some of

Lorene on national TV, NBC's "Home Show" with Arlene Francis, in 1958 - "I was on for 30 minutes, sharing pride in Alaska's push for statehood."

this longing for travel when she was named an "emergency stewardess" on a flight from Anchorage to Tokyo. "I was on a DC4, loaded down with enlisted men and one officer," Lorene recalls. "It took 22 hours with one stop in Shemya, for us to reach Tokyo."

That was just a taste for the travels that soon lay ahead. The world tour left Anchorage on a Northwest Airlines flight on March 15,

Mostly Music

1958, with eight Alaskans — including Jack and Lorene — on the travel roster. Brad Phillips went along, as did Lucy Cuddy, Lucy's sister, and the sister's husband. For the next two-and-a-half months, Lorene and the others would literally see the world, with Jack taking well-composed photos and slides, capturing their adventures. We see them in Japan, in Hong Kong and Thailand, perched on elephants in Cambodia, standing in front of the Taj Mahal in India, riding camels and boating down the Nile in Egypt, exploring the ruins of the Acropolis in Greece, journeying on to France and Italy, Switzerland, Germany, England and Holland, and the World's Fair in Brussels. What amuses Lorene greatly about these travel photos is that the women are seen always wearing dresses. "We always had skirts on –- never slacks –- no matter what the adventure." So there she is, sitting as gracefully as possible, side-saddle in her dresses, on both the camel and the elephant, and with the same hat in both photos. "That hat saw the world," Lorene says, laughing.

Toward the end of the 1958 world tour, Lorene and Jack look decidedly like a fine Dutch couple, posing in Volendam, Holland.

At one point in her life, Lorene had thought of teaching her way around the world. She calls this organized trip "a lot better idea," and adds, "It was marvelous!" Lorene confides that if she could wish for one more thing she could have added to her bag of tricks, or her abundant life experiences, it would be a pilot's license. "I've really no regrets," she states, "but that is the one thing I've always dreamed of doing — learning to fly. Just think where I could have gone!"

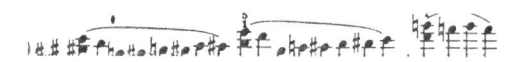

When Lorene again set down in Anchorage after this whirlwind tour, she realized that The Hat Box needed more of her attention. "I would have loved to have sold the shop at this point and gone into the travel business with Brad Phillips, as he had suggested. But a buyer for my shop was not to be found. I decided to drop the TV show. Theda Comstock took over in 1959. She had a lot of experience."

It was not as if Lorene had a lot of empty time on her hands. Back in 1955, she became a member of the original board of directors of the Alaska Festival of Music, founded by Mary Hale. (Lorene remembers that Mary and her husband, Dr. George Hale, had moved to Anchorage in 1949. "Mary was a public school music teacher, and sang in my Presbyterian Church choir.") Lorene served on that board until 1975. She was a member of Anchorage Community Theatre's board of directors from 1958 to 1963 and was active in the Soroptimists Club, holding all offices and becoming a life member.

Lorene also carried on with her hat buying trips to both New York and L.A., and gave what she called "Hat Chats" for organizations of military wives and other women's groups. "Two models went with me, a blond and a brunette, and I took along a selection of hats, scarves, handbags and other accessories that all tied together," Lorene explains. A large photo with a caption in the Anchorage Daily News, November 6, 1959, features these hat chats. The caption reads, "'HAT CHAT' by Mrs. Jack Harrison of The Hat Box was the featured program Wednesday when the Petroleum Wives Club held its November luncheon meeting. Held at the Penguin Club, Twelfth and Gambell, the regular gathering drew wives of employees of oil combined and related industries. Mrs. Harrison displayed new fall and winter chapeaus to illustrate her talk." All eyes are on Mrs. Harrison, depicted at the head of the linen-covered tables, and hats are perched on the heads of all in attendance!

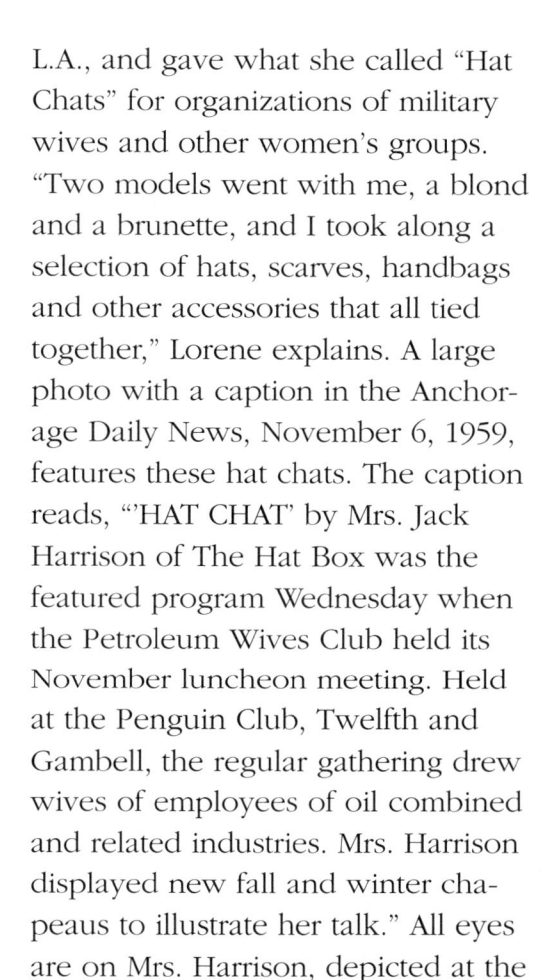

Lorene's life was more than full.

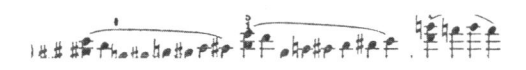

Around the World with Alaskans
1958 — Lorene and Jack are off on a world tour, arranged by Brad Phillips.

This is the world traveling party, just landed in Tokyo, Japan - Included in the photo are Jack and Lorene on the far right, with Brad Phillips in the dark glasses and Selma Smith, Lucy Cuddy and Mrs. Kennicot, among others.

Here are Jack and Lorene on a sampan going to Aberdeen at Hong Kong with their Chinese guide and Brad Phillips.

Yes, that's Jack and Lorene, off for an elephant ride at Angkor Wat, Cambodia on the Malay Peninsula.

Mostly Music

Cambodian Figures - Lorene notes, "There were many, many such figures in Cambodia and Thailand."

From elephants, to camels, Jack and Lorene got around! Here they are seen perched on camels, trekking off to see the ancient pyramids near Cairo, Egypt.

Lorene, on the right, and other travelers are examining ruins in New Dehli, India.

Lorene Harrison

The Alaska group poses with their guide in New Delhi, India.

The Alaska travelers pose once again, this time in front of what Lorene says is "surely one of the most beautiful structures in the world," the Taj Mahal in India.

Easter Sunday, 1958— Lorene recalls this was a very hot day, on the Nile River at Luxor, Eygpt. "One of the ladies in our group fainted from the heat."

Mostly Music

Lorene, Jack and Selma Smith, a school teacher from Anchorage, are seated in a carriage in front of the Hotel Winter Palace in Luxor, Egypt.

Once in Italy, the Alaskan travelers saw the Basilica of Saint Francis of Assissi.

The world trip took Jack and Lorene to Naples, Italy, seen here with their carriage driver.

Lorene Harrison

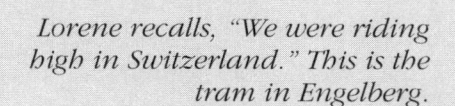

Lorene recalls, "We were riding high in Switzerland." This is the tram in Engelberg.

This is one of Lorene's favorite hotels on the tour, the Carlton-Hotel Tivoli in Lucerne, Switzerland.

Lorene remembers a whole day spent on this boat, journeying from Switzerland to Cologne, Germany.

Mostly Music

Lorene Harrison

Chapter Thirteen
The 1960s — Community Involvement, Chaperoning, '64 Earthquake, BPW Award

A first issue of a publication called the "Alaska Blue Book" came out in 1963, a kind of "who's who" in state organizations. It listed Lorene as one of Alaska's 49 outstanding private citizens. Not surprisingly, her listing of activities, civic and cultural, fills many lines. Typically, Lorene was not just a member of these organizations; she was an officer or on the board of directors. Added to her cultural activities was membership on the board of directors of the Anchorage Mental Health Association and the trust and scholarship committee of Greater Anchorage, Inc. And her business endeavor, The Hat Box, continued. With this whirlwind of lively activity, it would be easy to forget that by the middle of this decade, Lorene herself was in her 60s!

By 1960, The Hat Box was in "Bright New Quarters," according to a feature article in the *Anchorage Daily News* (March 26, 1960) – newly relocated to Third and E streets, in the Westward Hotel. Catching us up-to-date, the article states, "In her new shop, she has a special department for brides, including fancy lingerie and night wear. Another room is devoted to bridesmaids' and flower girls' dresses. And Lorene is now stocking dresses for the mother of the bride, to offer a complete line."

Mention is made of the fact that the bridal line was added to The Hat Box when daughter Pegge was making her wedding plans back in 1953. Not to overlook the hats in the newly expanded shop, the article also notes that Lorene "estimates she'll have about 2,000 hats available for Easter selections." Additional space at the back provided storage room for the stacks upon stacks of hat boxes. In a photo accompanying the article, we see Lorene and daughter, Carol Anne, admiring the latest in spring millinery creations, an elaborate Easter bonnet, in the "Designer Room" of the shop. It is noted that Carol Anne had been "her mother's first model" on Lorene's television show.

Love of people, of travel, and of fashion combined in 1962 in a new pursuit for Lorene. She became state chaperone for the Miss Alaska Pageant and continued in this role until 1970. Lorene feels she has always led a kind of charmed life — "being in the right place at the right time," she calls it, "and this designation was just another by-product of that good fortune." Alaska had been granted statehood three years earlier, back on January 3, 1959, so was now eligible for the

Lorene combined her love of people with her love of travel in 1962 when she became a state chaperone for the Miss Alaska Pageant. Here she is in one of her gowns that she would wear to the Miss America pageant in Atlantic City - front of the gown …

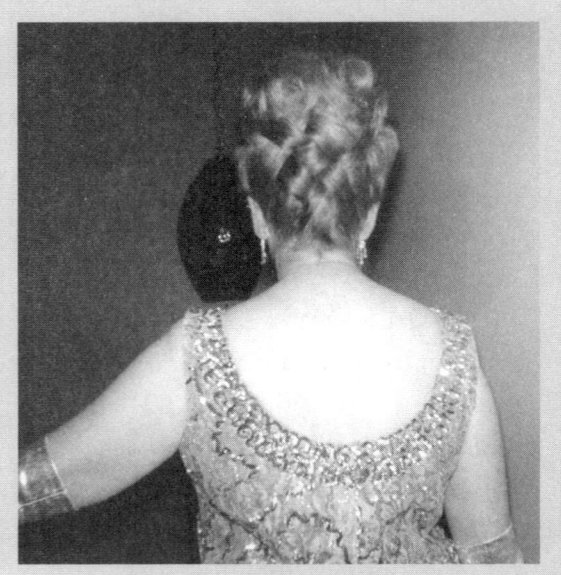

… and the back of the gown for Atlantic City.

state-by-state competition. In keeping with a pattern in Lorene's life, compensation for these chaperoning efforts came in the form of a wealth of experiences, not money, as Lorene was a volunteer. "It was very educational, a service," Lorene states. "I've always liked helping young women."

Lorene loves reliving memories from these eight years as a Miss Alaska chaperone. "I'd coordinate my hat buying trips east in late August, then on to Atlantic City for the pageants in early September. Those years were absolutely a highlight for me. The girls filled my home with laughter and liveliness as I worked with them to get ready for the competitions."

By now, Lorene's two daughters were married and living away from what had been their family home growing up. Lorene became known as "Grandma Hat" to their children. In 1963, Lorene and Jack were divorced. ("Jack remarried at once," Lorene states. "I think he felt he had always been in my shadow. He died five years later of arterio sclerosis and its complications.")

These difficult memories and the emptiness of Lorene's home with daughters grown and gone were softened by her work with the young women competing as Miss Alaska. Lorene worked with them on what she calls "social graces," helped them polish their talent, which she terms "the most impor-

Here is Lorene in another of the evening gowns she wore in Atlantic City as the Anchorage chaperone from 1962-70. (She is seen here with a chaperone from another state.)

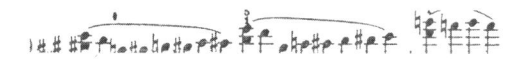

tant part of the competition," assisted them in choosing their gowns and other pieces of their wardrobe. All of these Miss Alaskas lived with Lorene in her home for the entire summer, getting ready for the national pageant. Lorene even converted a part of her home into what became her Miss Alaska Room, or the pink room. "It was on the lower floor, all decorated in pink — the walls, the ceiling, and the carpeting," Lorene remembers. Mothers of the contestants and some of the judges for the Miss Alaska competition also stayed in Lorene's home.

Lorene's "first Miss Alaska" - Mary Dee Fox, 1962, in her gown for the Miss America competition in Atlantic City.

At that time, these young women were called "beauty queens." To this day, Lorene hears from many of them and maintains close friendships with some. Two of them, Mary Dee Fox and Colleen Pettit Johansen, shared openly what they consider lifelong learning gleaned from their relationship with Lorene as both chaperone, surrogate mother, and friend — what could be termed "the Lessons of Lorene."

Lorene calls Mary Dee Fox "my first Miss Alaska." Back in 1962, Mary Dee won the Miss Fur Rendezvous title, considered a preliminary to the Miss Alaska competition. "I had absolutely no talent — not a stitch," Mary Dee says today, reflecting back on her "reign." Those words, "not a stitch," have an ironic ring to them now. "Believe it or not, I actually sewed on the stage in Atlantic City. Sewing a basic sleeveless sheath, and then a cape that could double as a skirt — that was my talent. That, and reciting a poem about Alaska written for me by Ruben Gaines, a radio personality from KFQD. He called me 'Queenie.' Lorene worked with me from April to September to get me ready. I was only 18, and she taught me everything. She taught me how to walk in high heels, how to stand tall, how to memorize my poem and how to annunciate. I was terribly shy. Back in 1962, we couldn't go anywhere without our chaperone."

Mary Dee continues, "Lorene was going through a difficult time right then, with the divorce, and we really bonded. She's so special to me. Lorene is still my very best friend."

Mary Dee remembers that Larry Beck, Alaskan writer and entertainer, would put together an album for each of the Miss Alaska contestants, about themselves and the state. "He became a kind of ambassador for Alaska, traveling all over the United States, writing poems and songs about Alaska, putting on skits. He called Lorene his surrogate mother," Mary Dee recalls. (Exhausted from his efforts and saddened that he had not accomplished all he had set out to do for himself and the state, Larry committed suicide in 1990. Lorene was the last person from his hometown of Anchorage that he talked to before his death. In a book he published, full of his stories and poetry, he had written as an autograph to Lorene: "For my best friend and Alaska's living legend – with love – Larry Beck, August 10, 1986.")

Another of these "beauty queens" with whom Lorene has maintained an ever increasing bond of friendship is Colleen Pettit Johansen. In

To this day, Mary Dee and Lorene are the closest of friends - "She's so special to me," Mary Dee says. Here Lorene stands in for Mary Dee's mother (who was ill) at Mary Dee's recent wedding.

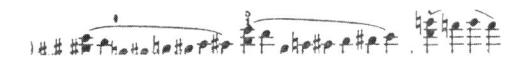

1967, Colleen was named Miss Alaska Centennial, part of a celebration sponsored by the state to commemorate the one hundredth anniversary of the purchase of Alaska from Russia. With Lorene as her

chaperone, the two traveled coast-to-coast, making appearances. "It was summer and the temperature was often in the 90s. There I was in my parka and mukluks, with a crown of fur and ivory on my head," Colleen remembers, laughing.

Larry Beck (known as the "Bard of Alaska") and Lorene share a hug in 1985 - Larry called Lorene "my best friend." She was the last person in Anchorage he talked to before his 1990 suicide.

Two appearances that most stand out in Colleen's memories happened in Auburn, New York and Washington, D.C. "Auburn is the birthplace of William Henry Seward, who saw to the purchase of Alaska as Secretary of State. It was called 'Seward's Icebox' by some at the time," Colleen explains. "There was an enormous Alaska Centennial celebration in that town in 1967.

Auburn considered itself the 'Honorary Capital of Alaska,' and Mrs. William Henry Seward III was a part of the commemorative festivities." (Lorene remembers this Mrs. Seward well. "She was a grand old lady, I'll tell you.")

After a quick side trip to the World's Fair in Montreal, the two, Lorene and Colleen, went on to D.C., where they met with then President Lyndon Johnson for 20 minutes in the Oval Office, and had photos taken with him in the White House garden. "We also had dinner with Senator Bob Bartlett and Congressman Howard Pollock," Colleen remembers.

"Lorene and I became such great buddies, traveling side-by-side all that time," Colleen summarizes.

Her list of Lessons of Lorene is lengthy and amusing. "She taught me not to eat french fries with my

Lorene Harrison

Colleen Pettit, Miss Alaska Centennial in 1967 - Colleen remembers traveling coast to coast that hot summer "in my parka and mukluks!"

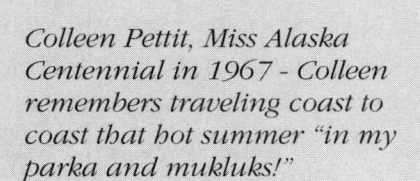

Colleen plays up her Alaska home, traveling as Miss Alaska Centennial.

Colleen Pettit and Lorene in Ottawa, Canada - "We were guests of the Canadian government at <u>their</u> Centennial" — 1967.

fingers. 'That's a fork food,' she said. She taught me how to pack. 'Roll your clothing, don't fold it.' She taught me to write a thank you note. 'Don't eat it, wear it, or use it if it's given to you — unless you are willing to write a thank you note.' She taught me to giggle, to have a sense of humor, and more importantly, to be positive. Don't complain. 'As a man thinketh, so is he,' and 'Circumstance does not make the man; it reveals the man to himself.' She taught me to be punctual. Lorene told me she was never tardy to school, and never absent except for typhoid fever in second grade and a cousin's death in sixth grade. She showed me that travel broadens you — in more ways than one. We both loved ice cream!"

A tragic memory comes from the Miss Alaska pageant of 1964. Chosen as Miss Alaska that year was Karol Hommon. Lorene remembers her as being "very, very pretty, full of personality, and the only girl I chaperoned who got a special award at the national Miss America pageant." The award was presented for her talent — "so exceptional that she received a $2000 prize toward her college education," Lorene remembers. "She was an acrobatic dancer, and we had an igloo constructed out of something like Styrofoam for her to work into her tumbling routine."

One month after the pageant, in October of 1964, she died.

July 17, 1967, Alaska's Centennial year - the White House garden - left to right: Lorene, Colleen's chaperone; Howard Pollock, U.S. Congressman from Alaska; Colleen Pettit, Miss Alaska Centennial; Lyndon B. Johnson, U.S. President; Bob Bartlett, Alaska U.S. Senator.

"She had gone off to Smith College in Massachusetts for her sophomore year," Lorene states. "It was her first year there, since she had gone to Alaska Methodist University, now Alaska Pacific University, for her freshman year. She didn't even tell her new roommate about her participation in the Miss America pageant just weeks before. She wanted to make friends on her own merits, not because of some national attention." Karol, her Smith College roommate and some other friends had gone on an early fall picnic to Sugar Loaf Mountain, near the campus, taking their books along. "Foolishly, they had put their blankets down beyond the warning signs, 'Do not go beyond this point,' along a cliff," Lorene recalls. "Karol tripped on the edge of the blanket, fell over the rim of the cliff, and grabbed onto a sapling, trying to keep herself from falling. She held her friend's hand as long as she could, but couldn't keep holding on and went down 200 feet."

Karol's mother, Dorothy Hommon, worked for Lorene at The Hat Box. "Karol had lived for a short while after the fall. Her mother called me at the shop and told me, 'Something awful

Karol Hommon, Miss Alaska 1964, crowns her successor, Mary Nidiffer - "Karol had won a $2,000 prize for her talent, acrobatic dancing, at the Miss America Pagent. Her sudden death was so tragic."

has happened. I can't come to work.' Smith College had just phoned her about the accident. I went right over to her parents' home, along with Karol's boyfriend from Anchorage, Walter Afield. We just held each other."

Mostly Music

Walter Afield, now a psychiatrist, married with a family and living in Tampa, Florida, is on Lorene's long list of people she still holds close, so many years after meeting them. "I still hear from him." It's a kind of theme song of Lorene's life. She adds, as if surprising even herself, "See how I've kept in touch with so many people? It's so interesting!"

Another of the Miss Alaskas still very much in touch with Lorene is Nancy Wellman, now Nancy Wellman DeLeon and living in Fairbanks. "She won the title of Miss Alaska in 1965," Lorene explains. "Her talent was singing." Always one to organize and plan, to the very end of any project — even a life — Lorene adds, "Nancy has agreed to sing 'The Lord's Prayer' at my memorial service." Then she adds with a laugh, "Meanwhile, she visits me several times a year."

Not to be overlooked are the "Lessons of Lorene" learned by her own two daughters, in addition to what she taught to the young women she chaperoned in the 1960s. Carol Anne remembers lessons in the kitchen. "Mom cooked with everything – and I learned to eat everything!" She begins a long list of food memories. "Mom made peas and dumplings, put peanut butter on carrots, made fried eggplant and fried corn meal. She made a ham gravy, and put lima beans and ham on corn bread. Oh, that was so good! I remember her clover leaf rolls in muffin tins. Mom made thousands of those. I still have that recipe. One of the salesmen travel-

Colleen with Robert Bitar, Consul of Lebanon, in Portland, Oregon - "Lorene taught me that travel is an education. She taught me so much."

Nancy Wellman, Miss Alaska 1965, performs in Atlantic City. Lorene says, "She has a beautiful soprano voice. I've already asked to her sing at my memorial service some day!"

Nancy Wellman (now Nancy DeLeon and living in Fairbanks), and Lorene still get together. Here they are at a restaurant for dinner in the summer of 1996.

The cast, writer and composer of Toyon of Alaska, the Centennial commemorative production, with Lorene as chair of the music committee. Pictured here are, back row, left to right: John Drykers, Gov. Walter Hickel, Earlene Plowman, Leon Lishner, writer Frank Brink, and Howard Fried. Front row: unidentified on the left; composer Willard Straight on the right.

ing through town in the early 1940s had a contest with me when I was about 8, to see who could eat the most rolls. His name was Bill Douglass. Together we ate 23!" Having watched her mother, Carol Anne learned to cook, and while her mother had The Hat Box, she often prepared the family's dinners.

Pegge still has a little notebook kept by her mother listing what was served, to whom and when. (She flips to her 10th birthday, February 15, 1942, to discover that Lorene had prepared fried chicken, mashed potatoes, beet Jello, rolls and vegetables.) She estimates that during the war years, the family had GI's as guests for over half of their meals. One entry in 1942 shows that Lorene made a moose roast with spuds, cranberries and rolls for the family and guest soldiers.

Pegge takes the lessons from her mother out of the kitchen to a more philosophical realm. "She taught me to be optimistic, to be mindful of my health, to have faith – and not to hit my sister!"

Upon returning to Anchorage from chaperoning Colleen Pettit as Miss Alaska Centennial, Lorene continued work on the Centennial by assuming the duties of head of the state's centennial music committee, and was given a grant of $100,000 to put together a commemorative production. She got Frank Brink and Willard Straight to write a musical drama about the purchase of Alaska from Russia. Called "Toyon of Alaska," by all accounts it was a great success, taken on tour to many Alaska communities. In Anchorage, it was put on in the West High auditorium from July 7 to July 11 of the centennial year.

It was two years into these chaperoning duties, or in 1964, that Alaska experienced a jolt that will continue to spin stories as long as there are those around who lived through it to tell them. Lorene calls the 1964 earthquake that hit Anchorage and other areas of the state "a story – a book – in itself." She adds, "No one's story of life in 1964 in Anchorage would be complete without the 'Where were you when it hit?' memories."

Lorene's recollections are vivid, frightening, but not without some humor. "It was just before Easter, Good Friday, the busiest day for my shop — always my Big Hat Day. Well, that year it would have a big surprise finish!" At 5:26 p.m. on Friday, March 27, 1964, an earthquake measuring 9.2 Mw rumbled through the city.

"I had left The Hat Box after that busy day about 5 p.m. I was going home to see if the painters had finished some work in my home. Once there, I let my little dog Emily out into the fenced yard, then put some newspapers in the tub in the bathroom so I could stand on them to hang up a new shower curtain. I was standing there with my boots on when I felt a little quiver. It gave me pause, but I held the curtain back up again and fastened one side. Then things began to really rock. The ground was heaving and groaning. I didn't dare move, just held onto the window sill and the curtain rod. I believe I hung on like that for five minutes, but it seemed like forever."

We can pick up this story from what is a primary source, almost an immediate accounting, a letter written by Lorene on April 10, 1964, just a few days after the earthquake, to her many concerned friends and family members.

The letter begins:

My Dear Friends,

Already I have had well over one hundred anxious letters of inquiry as to my safety and well-being, so please forgive me for sending out mimeographed letters. There is so very much to be done here in trying to get back into business, trying to be helpful to dear friends who have lost their homes and everything they owned, that this seems the best way to let all you wonderful people know that the Dodds (daughter Carol Anne's family) and I all fared very well through this dramatic experience.

It is difficult to explain the effect of the tremendous power of nature as exhibited in the earthquake of March 27, Good Friday, 1964 — the greatest force ever to be felt in the Northern Hemisphere – as I stood in my bathtub trying to hang a new curtain, in Anchorage, Alaska at 5:26 p.m.!" She goes on to describe those first few *"bumps"* and *"sways"* as she hung on to the rod. *"I remember thinking, as I heard my table and floor lamps fall, my china and crystal crash, that I had better stay where I was (standing in the tub), for at least nothing could fall on me there but the roof – and then my cosmetics from the glass shelves fell into the tub at my feet. I think one gets rather numb just feeling the utter helplessness of trying to compete with the unlimited force of nature. Flashing through my mind was the safety of Carol Anne and her three little ones, and of the five sales girls I had left at my store 30 minutes earlier.*

As soon as things quieted down, I stepped out of the tub, through the hall and living room and rushed out the side door into the street. My neighbor, white as a sheet, pointed across the Park Strip on one block where a new six-story apartment house almost completed (The Four Seasons), to be the most 'plush' in Anchorage, had just fallen into a great fissure of the earth and was a pile of rubble and cement dust. Five houses directly across from me had also sunk about 20 feet – also two cars parked in front of the houses. Everything was deathly quiet – no panic, no screaming – but also no heat, no gas, no electricity, no telephone service, no water, no sewer facilities, and no telegraph system; therefore, no immediate comprehension of the tremendous damage done to the Anchorage area and certainly no thought of the devastation being done to Seward, Kodiak, Valdez, and smaller towns on the coast due mostly to the vast tidal waves.

I threw on my coat and overshoes, put the dog into my car which was in the garage attached to the house; but the car had jumped and slid in such a manner as to take some maneuvering to get it out of the garage. Just then a pilot drove by that Carol Anne used to fly with, so he stopped. He was going to the hotel to pick up a stewardess for a flight (not knowing that the terminal was completely destroyed and the tower had fallen, killing one man). I hopped in the car with him to go to my store to see how the (sales)girls were. We had to detour many times as deep fissures were in the roads and buildings had fallen down in them. Three of my girls were still at the store –– out in the street –– knowing I would come. Three doors at the store had sprung shut and wouldn't open, but the front door sprung open and wouldn't close. Two patrolmen came by and said we would have to get off the street at once as minor tremors were still occurring, that there would be a guard at my corner, and to get home and stay off the streets.

I got in Alyce's car (my floor manager) and drove to my house with Emily in it, and we headed for Spenard to the Dodds. There was a note on the door saying, 'Mother – all O.K. Gone to the field' (meaning Cordova Airlines hangar). So we headed there – past guards who were already keeping people out of the badly damaged areas. Carol Anne, Bob, and the three children were in the car with blankets, three bottles of formula for Baby Edward, and a box of graham crackers! No one had, of course, had dinner. We all sat out in the wide open spaces *in the two cars for a couple of hours, sparingly using the heater to conserve gas, and listening to our conelrad emergency radio station.*

When the quake hit, Carol Anne had Edward in her arms, so she grabbed a blanket and took him out in the backyard and sat him on the snow. Kelly came under her own power (five years old) but Diane got stuck in a door and was pretty frantic as Carol Anne pulled her through. They had to crawl out to the baby, the ground was rolling so badly. Bob had been at the airlines office and had dashed in his car the half mile home for the family.

We all decided to go to some good friends of the Dodds who had a fireplace. We spent the night on the floor, daveno and chairs in their living room – trembling as each tremor came, listening on the transistor radio to the news and warnings to stay off the roads, and I must say, we were all pretty jittery. Andy made some sandwiches about midnight, which we relished with Coke.

It was afternoon of the next day that we all ventured to our own homes. What a mess were my floors – very nearly every piece of china that I had in my generous kitchen cupboards was in tiny pieces on the kitchen floor. My refrigerator door had come open, food fallen out, and the door closed again. But a few of my bone china cup and saucer collection which was on open shelves didn't appear to have even moved. My stereo speakers were flat on the floor, every lamp in the house had broken reflectors and bulbs. In my music room, my Acrosonic piano, heavy daveno and studio table were all centered in the middle of the floor, but all upright.

But, our losses were very light compared to the 500 or more families who saw their homes go churning down the banks of Cook Inlet from the wonderful view of the bluffs, or those that dropped into crevasses, or those who lost dear ones. The destruction is simply unbelievable –– and most of it in five minutes' time. Our main business district for two blocks is in shambles –– no doubt you saw pictures of this. Someone said Anchorage looked like the hand of God had been there. The structures of no churches nor hospitals were hurt; but the two blocks filled with bars were demolished! Very few people had earthquake insurance as it is so awfully expensive. There were no fires nor water in Anchorage. We hope for low-interest, long-term loans from the government or SBA (Small Business Association) to help the businesses get reestablished. Some money for roads, utilities, etc.

seems to be already forthcoming from Washington, D.C. and the Alaska legislature.

Many women with small children flew stateside within the first few days. Bob was able to get a pass for Carol Anne so she and the children left for Portland to be with Bob's mother, within 24 hours of the quake. She didn't get to see many of the heartbreaking sights. With no water and heat, it's pretty rugged. I'm so glad she could go. I'm so tired of 'burping' Clorox. The military stationed tanks of water at various places, but we had to boil it and put four drops of Clorox in for every quart. One tank, and a tent with an emergency rations kitchen and hot coffee was on the Park Strip directly across the street from me.

For Easter, I had four guests –– we had cold ham and canned potato salad on paper plates. There has been no shortage of food, as the store shelves and warehouses were filled. Within a week, almost all utilities have been restored except gas and water in a few areas.

Many water and sewer mains were broken, as well as the gas lines. People with fireplaces took in other families; the Red Cross was active; Civil Defense marvelous; military indispensable, and the Salvation Army, superb! Many families were separated that first long, long night with no communication whatsoever and sentries to keep people off the roads because of crevasses. They say the earth will continue to settle for as much as two years!

Lorene with two of her Hat Box employees and close friends, Alyce Robinson (in the middle) and Fran Mues. Lorene says, "This photo was taken in 1985 of my two wonderful employees with me. Both weathered the 1964 earthquake with me and the shop!"

Lorene Harrison

The Hat Box, located on the northeast corner of the Anchorage-Westward Hotel, had a big crack near the corner, plaster damage and minor cracks inside. But it is structurally sound, they say. However, I cannot do business there until the new 14-story tower of the hotel has been further reinforced. The manager estimates eight weeks, so it may be 12! I have rented one hotel room on the street level, and we've moved as much of my merchandise as it will hold -- a precious small percentage -- into it. My employees and I can go into The Hat Box for merchandise, but cannot have customers there. I was out of business for ten days, looking for a location, awaiting engineers' reports, etc. Most business people are very optimistic – 'We'll build better for a better city,' etc. But, we have to have money to build and pay for supplies and merchandise.

Three things amaze me -- first, the total amount of destruction and devastation; second, the extremely small number of lives lost in such a sizeable disaster; and third, the organization and speed with which reconstruction is being carried on.

I have so very much for which to be thankful. All I lost can be replaced with money. I've never been afraid of work, and I work best with a challenge. This is not the greatest problem I've ever had, and I know I can lick it.

One article in our Times summed up thus, and I like it -- 'The figure of the dead is astonishingly low. Why? Some explained it in terms of Alaska's sparse population, small towns, broad streets, and low buildings. Others found the answer on their knees.'

It has truly been an 'earth shaking' experience, one I would not want to repeat, but it makes one just grateful to be alive.

*   As ever,*
*   Lorene*

As time went by, humorous recollections emerged, even from the dust of these most trying circumstances. Lorene reflects back on one scene, just outside The Hat Box when she went there immediately after the quake. "A woman had been inside the shop, trying on an Easter bonnet, sitting posed in front of a mirror, when the ground began to sway. She jumped up, the bonnet still perched on her head, and fled out the door. 'Wait! Wait!' Fran Mues, one of my dedicated sales staff, yelled, flying out the door after her, flagging her arms as the earth rocked. 'Do you want to buy that hat?' 'I'll be back later,' the panicked customer managed to reply, and handed her back the hat."

Ever mindful of her professional responsibilities, Lorene wrote to her millinery suppliers in New York, asking them for their patience as she got back on her business feet. A few weeks after the earthquake, the following headline appeared in a New York City newspaper, "Hat Industry Survives All Obstacles – Even Earthquakes." The article reads, "The millinery industry will survive all obstacles – even earthquakes. This had been proved by Mrs. Lorene Harrison, whose shop, The Hat Box, in Anchorage, Alaska, received a great deal of damage during the March earthquake. Mrs. Harrison refuses to be defeated by the destructive forces of nature, and recently, she opened for business once again. While repairs were being made, she operated out of room 129 in the Anchorage-Westward Hotel. She is particularly grateful to her suppliers for their confidence."

Lorene remembers one amusing incident while using the hotel room as the temporary Hat Box. "We were using the room in the basement of the hotel, running back and forth from that room to the shop, to get things. People were still getting married, you know, earthquake or no earthquake, and they were coming in to try on bridal gowns. A bride-to-be had come in to buy her wedding dress, and Alyce Robinson, my employee,

Life goes on after the earthquake and Anchorage begins a vigorous rebuilding campaign. Here, in 1965, Lorene, Miss Alaska, Mary Ruth Nidiffer, are escorted by a gendarme, flown in from France by Walter Hickel, for the grand opening of his Captain Cook Hotel. "Walter Hickel rolled out the red carpet for that evening! It was under our feet as we walked from a limo he had sent to my house, and into the new hotel!"

had gone to The Hat Box to bring back several gowns for her to try on. We used the bathroom in the basement as a dressing room, but someone was in there. Alyce spotted a room just down the hall with no one in it. 'Let's try there,' she said, and she and the bride-to-be went inside. She'd just pulled a gown on over her head when all this dirty linen came down a shoot, landing all over both of them." Post-earthquake was obviously a makeshift time, not without its funny, lighter moments.

Lorene began running a series of ads in the *Anchorage Daily Times*, to let the public know she was still open for business. A 4-inch by 4-inch ad placed on April 13, 1964, reads, "The Hat Box has no hard hats but hats for hard heads (the kind that stay in Alaska and rebuild) – New location, Room 129 Anchorage Westward Hotel – phone BR5-5301." A week-and-a-half later, on April 23 in the *Times*, a large photo was run, showing Lorene's big art deco sign, with its neon letters and graphic hat box design, being hoisted by a worker, back over the shop entrance. The caption reads,

"Lewis Lestock, wearing a hard hat which probably didn't come from The Hat Box, helps to install the shop's sign in a new location at the corner of Third Avenue and E Street. The shop was displaced by

February, 1965 - Lorene is given a testimonial dinner by the Business and Professional Women's Club - "Looking at the photo, you can tell it was a big surprise! You see my face as Ruth Briggs, a longtime special friend, acted as mistress of ceremonies. Red roses and a beautiful silver fruit bowl were given to me."

the March 27 earthquake. The hard hats are the latest fashion style for many Anchorage area workers."

Some of the threads of life are not interrupted, even by a major disaster. Lorene's business obviously went on, as did her string of awards. On February 2, 1965, the Business and Professional Women's Club held a surprise testimonial dinner for her in recognition of her community service. Ruth Briggs served as mistress of ceremonies. Presentations were made by Fred Chei, then president of the Greater Anchorage Chamber of Commerce; George Sharrock, the immediate past mayor; and Elmer Rasmuson, the current mayor. Calling his presentation, "Lorene, the Inspiration," Elmer Rasmuson stated, "Your industry – your accomplishments – your dreams – your vitality – your warm-heartedness and bright countenance – have truly made you an inspiration to all of us who know you. You manage to keep your feet on the ground and your personal and multitudinous civic enterprises, and yet you keep your heart and head in the clouds as you pursue your cultural endeavor. The city of Anchorage is a better place because of you."

In 1967, she was made an honorary member of Delta Kappa Gamma, teachers' sorority, and that same year, Lorene received a service award from the Alaska Purchase Centennial Commission for her work as the performing and fine arts chair of centennial festivities.

One of the honors that most delights Lorene was a surprise, spurred on by Norma Goodman, another of Anchorage's "first women of television." In August of 1968, Lorene was feted on the "Norma Goodman Show." "What a lovely surprise," Lorene recalls. The August 6 edition of the *Anchorage Daily News* carried a photo of Lorene, smiling behind a huge spray of red roses and baby's breath, with the caption,

1968 — Another surprise honor, this time on "The Norma Goodman" television show - "It was a real surprise party, a kind of 'This Is Your Life' presentation. My family including grandchildren, and business and family friends were all there to surprise me! And there were all kinds of lovely gifts."

"Anchorage's Hedda Hopper – Mrs. Lorene Harrison." The story tells us that Lorene was a surprise guest of honor on Norma Goodman's "Hostess House" on KTVA and that the show turned out to be "a hometown version" of a popular nationally televised show, "This Is Your Life." "Lorene, owner of The Hat Box, celebrates 20 years in the millinery business on August 22, but she'll be on a swing to the East Coast then (New York for a buying trip and on to Atlantic City for the Miss America pageant as official hostess for Miss Alaska Jane Haycroft)." The article repeats the story of Lorene's first day of business at The Hat Box when she sold out her entire supply of hand-crafted hats in just hours, hats she remembered as being small and often covered with veils or feathers. Included in the surprise television show were members of Lorene's family "along with many friends of Lorene's and civic officials who cited her for outstanding contributions – especially in the music field – to Anchorage."

Another continuing thread, throughout the earthquake aftermath years, was Lorene's generosity and concern for others. In 1967, a Dr. Paul Jensen, Danish-born professor teaching in Oregon, came to Anchorage to

The new St. Lawrence Island bridal gown - "I gave this bridal ensemble to the St. Mary's church for all the girls to be married in." Lorene had caught word of "the one tired bridal dress" that was recirculating among the island's brides in the 1960s.

address the 13th Western Alaska Regional Teachers' Conference. The local newspaper referred to him as an educator who was "keenly interested in Native culture and a professor who speaks some Eskimo." While making an Anchorage television appearance, he told the story of "the St. Lawrence Island wedding dress." He also stopped by Lorene's shop. It seems that there was only one wedding gown on the island at the time, and thus any bride was forced into wearing it, no matter what her personal tastes, letting it in or out and the hem up and down to accommodate her size and shape – to the point that it was well frazzled. This went on for 10 years.

Always ready to meet a need, Lorene sent off a letter to the minister in Gambell on St. Lawrence Island.

"Oh, he has a great time on his motorcycle, his favorite mode of transportation," Lorene says of longtime friend and former Anchorage Symphony conductor, Maurice Dubonnet. Here they 'move on out' in 1987. Lorene was visiting her nephew's family in Arizona, where Maurice now lives.

March 27, 1967
Dear Rev. Gall,

Very likely you have already heard through one means or another that Dr. Paul Jensen from Oregon came into my store a few weeks ago and told me the sad tale of the worn-out bridal gown on St. Lawrence Island!

His sincerity...plus the fact that I have in my store the 'Bridal Corner' led to the selection on the spot of a bridal gown and veil to (expedite) the well-deserved retirement of the one in use for ten years!...

I do hope this will answer your immediate need, and I am so happy to have a part in this bit of excitement!

Yours very sincerely,
Mrs. Lorene Harrison

Back from Savoonga on St. Lawrence Island came a note of thanks from the Rev. Gall. Dated May 6, 1967, it reads, in part:

Quite some time ago we received your package containing a beautiful wedding gown, also a letter attached. For this most generous gift..., please accept our profound gratitude. How thoughtful and kind of you to do this, and I want you to know that it is deeply appreciated.

I am not sure what gown Dr. Jensen, whom we know, was referring to. I assume it was the one in Gambell. Here in Savoonga we have about half a dozen which belong to the Presbyterian Mission and which are being used now and then. There used to be more in Gambell also, but some of the gowns just did not come back after the wedding....

Your gift gown will stay in Gambell in care of the missionary there (I happen to serve the churches in both villages, Gambell and Savoonga)....

Most sincerely and gratefully yours,

> Rev. Alwin E. Gall
> St. Lawrence Island
> Gambell, Alaska

A photo of Lorene and Dr. Jensen, admiring the gift gown before its shipment to the island, appeared that spring in the Anchorage papers.

Sharing her home was another continuing thread in the fabric of Lorene's intricate life pattern all through the 1950s and '60s. The door to Lorene's home, Anchorage's "hospitality house," remained open, despite the earthquake damage it had sustained. One long-term guest was Maurice Dubonnet, who became the conductor of the Anchorage Symphony in 1968 and con-

Marilyn and Gary Smart - Gary is a pianist and composer; Marilyn a gifted soprano. "Frank Pinkerton was the president, I believe, that year of the Anchorage Arts Council and made the arrangement for the Smarts to come from Germany," Lorene says. "They became excellent friends of Maurice Dubonnet and myself. Gary wrote a piece called 'The Hat Box Rag' for me, to be performed with 'energy and good humor,' he noted. And it was - performed a very great deal! Maurice rides his motorcycle to visit Gary and Marilyn on his trips east from Arizona."

ducted that orchestra until 1981. He also conducted the symphony in Fairbanks. Lorene comments, "He lived at my house on the lower level

Mostly Music

Two of the "men of the lower level" who stayed in what became known as "Lorene's hospitality house" - Tom Atkinson, on the left, who moved in in 1965, and Hans Kirchner, who moved there in 1960. They are sitting with little terrier, Emily, between them.

"This is Tom with my very dear friend, May Nock, who lived next door to me for 15 years in the Park Place Condos."

for five years – in the 'pink room,' obviously after my days of chaperoning the Miss Alaskas. The symphony couldn't pay him. I told that organization, 'You can consider my providing his housing as my contribution to the symphony,' worth about $60 a month. I also took him back and forth from the airport, as he was so often flying to Fairbanks, to conduct the symphony and to teach at the university there."

In summarizing his contributions to the Anchorage Symphony, Lorene states, "Maurice brought the symphony from an exaggerated high school orchestra level to a metropolitan status. The community was so pleased by the difference he made; he was the first symphony conductor brought here from out-of-state."

It should come as no surprise to learn that Lorene still keeps in touch with him, as with so many others who have entered her life. "He's living in Mesa, Arizona," she explains. "He rides around on a motorcycle, his main form of transportation. He'd be 70-some years old now, and, oh, he has a great time. He's been known to ride from Arizona to Kansas, stopping there on his motorcycle to see one of my many favorite nephews."

Maurice is but one of many men who found a home on the lower level of Lorene's house. All except Maurice were renters, paying for their room and enjoying her good cooking as a bonus. Some came out of an immediate crisis in their lives, expecting to spend the night or at most a week – and stayed for years.

Lorene begins the tale of the men of the lower level by going back to 1952 and Bill Lindgren, whom she calls "a great guy and excellent friend to both me and to Jack." The Harrisons had met Bill at the Garden of Eatin', a restaurant constructed from a Quonset hut in the Spenard area. Bill was head of the food department for Alaska Airlines and had been renting a room in the Westward Hotel, living there until the hotel changed the policy of people actually living out of its rooms. "We ran into him one day in the early 1950s, and he told us he was looking for a place to stay. We invited him to our home; he was going to stay just until he found a place to live. He lived with us for 10 years," Lorene states, laughing.

Following along behind Bill, and staying in Lorene's lower level for

Hans Kirchner owned the quonset hut restaurant, the 'Garden of Eatin,' for many years.

two years that overlapped with Bill was Hans Kirchner. The Harrisons had been good friends of the Kirchners, who owned the Garden of Eatin'. When Hans and his wife divorced in 1960, Jack asked Lorene, "What would you think of Hans staying here?" And so Hans moved in, and Bill and Hans continued as tenants and very good friends. "In the summer of 1962,

Hans went off to Europe on a trip," Lorene explains. "That fall, in October, Jack had left home, before our divorce. While Hans was in Europe, Bill died – in December of 1962. My home was full of his friends and relatives for the funeral. Hans was so upset," Lorene adds.

Hans stayed with Lorene through 1964. "He was in my home the night of the earthquake, the night I spent in a car," Lorene recalls. "Eventually he moved to a mobile home just across from his restaurant, the Garden of Eatin'. He had long hours there and needed to sleep a couple of hours in the afternoons before getting dinners. My home was too noisy for him, with the construction of the third floor addition, and he couldn't sleep."

Next came a friend of Lorene's daughter, Carol Anne. Tom Atkinson had been married in 1964. On the day of the one-year anniversary of his marriage, Tom's wife and her father were killed in a car accident. "I didn't know him," Lorene states, "but he knew he couldn't stay in the apartment he had shared with his wife. Carol Anne told him, 'Go talk to my mother. She has a kind of rooming house.' This was the January right after Bill had died — one month later."

"Well, Tom moved in, and there was no way of telling how long he would need to stay. He stayed 18 years, from 1965 until 1983," Lorene states, laughing again at the way life had a knack of tossing long-term friends her way. "There were a couple of breaks in those 18 years," Lorene adds. "Tom had been married, moved out, and then divorced. He came into my store one day and asked, 'Can I move back in?' I said sure. We were such good friends, and he really looked out for me, took care of me so well."

Obviously, then, Tom's stay overlapped with some of the Miss Alaskas, and with Maurice Dubonnet, who moved in in 1969. Asked if this mixture of male tenants and female guests was ever confusing, Lorene replies, "No. Their stays really didn't cross over that much. And the men used the downstairs bathroom and the women the upstairs." With the third floor addition to her home in 1965, Lorene had ample room to accommodate and entertain her many guests.

Lorene's little terrier, Emily, loved all the company. "If Tom, Hans, Bill, or Maurice were at the door, Emily made no sound. She knew who was there and was glad they were home. If someone else came to the door, she let me know with loud, continuous barking! Emily lived 17 years, until November 1, 1970."

Another of "the men of the lower level," Tom Atkinson, had been a friend of Carol Anne's. When his wife died in a car accident, he moved in - and stayed for 18 years. "He was the most like a son that I've ever had," Lorene says.

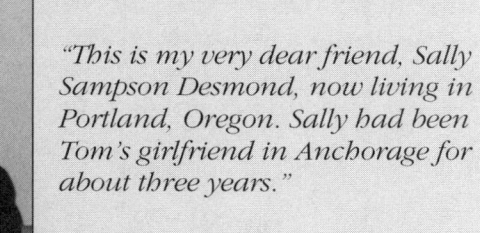

"This is my very dear friend, Sally Sampson Desmond, now living in Portland, Oregon. Sally had been Tom's girlfriend in Anchorage for about three years."

Lorene added the third floor to her home at 10th and N in 1965 - "the better to entertain you." Here some of her grandchildren sit in a corner of the new third-floor living room, looking out on Delaney Park.

Mostly Music

Lorene Harrison

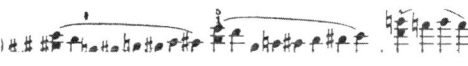

Chapter Fourteen
1970s — "I'm Tapering Off."

Lorene looks back on the decade of the 1970s as a time when "I eased off a bit." She, herself, was entering her 70s. To anyone else, at any age, her schedule would most likely appear daunting, characterized as anything but a "taking it easy" time.

In 1969, the Anchorage Arts Council had been set up, with Lorene doing all the preliminary correspondence for its establishment. For two years, 1970 to 1972, she served as the AAC vice president. "I was too busy to be president," she admits, "so I talked Ross Wood into being president."

Then in June of 1970, she was tour leader for a dozen local people, traveling through eight countries in Europe. "We flew over the pole to Copenhagen via SAS, then to Amsterdam, where we boarded a luxury bus on which we continued our travels."

Leading to more opportunities for travel, Lorene was named a member of the prestigious International Platform Association in 1971 and attended its convention in Washington, D.C. that August. She had been nominated for membership in this organization, which recognizes outstanding individuals in the public speaking or performance fields, by Lowell Thomas, Senior.

Mostly Music

June, 1970 - Lorene is a tour guide for a dozen Alaskans, traveling through eight European countries. "Here the maitre-de is showing me just how much spaghetti he is going to feed me!"

WInston Churchill III - with Mr. and Mrs. Kline - "Mr. Kline was president of the International Platform Association at this time. I spent a day touring the Churchills' lovely estate with other members of the International Platform Association convention.

"He was president of the International Platform Association at the time," Lorene states, "and had seen my work on my television show." She flew over to London with over one hundred members of the association, to present a gift, a bronze bust and head of Sir Winston Churchill, to his family. He had been one of the Platform Association's most distinguished members. She remembers meeting his grandson. "Sir Winston Churchill III was a charming gentleman. We spent a day with the Churchill family at their lovely estate. After a week in London, I flew back to New York to buy 'pretties' for my shop, then home again to Anchorage."

It was on that trip to Washington, D.C. for the International Platform Association's convention that

Lorene got to meet Jerry Connor, a friend with whom she had corresponded for some time, but someone she had not seen face-to-face until then. "Our lives seemed to be on parallel courses, more than just the fact that we were both members of the International Platform Association," Lorene states. "He was an inspirational writer and also ran a bridal consultant business, National Bridal Service. My employee, Alyce Robinson, had taken a correspondence course he had written, for certification as a professional bridal consultant, the first certified in Alaska, I believe. I had had much business correspondence with him, and that had grown into a long-distance friendship, so we were eager to have a chance to meet in Washington. We very much enjoyed our visit there, continued to write back and forth for several years, and he had planned to bring his wife to Anchorage to visit me. But that was still a very upsetting time for me, full of stress from the divorce. I asked Jerry and his wife to postpone their visit, and they never did get to come."

In 1981, Jerry wrote a book of profiles of 14 people he felt were his most inspirational friends, a

Lorene with a White House guard — "I was attending an International Platform Association convention."

"While at the Washington, D.C. convention, I met Jerry Connor. We had corresponded by mail for some time prior to meeting face-to-face. He ran a bridal consultant business and was an inspirational writer, including me in his book on inspirational friends!"

book he dedicated to his wife and titled "Great Personalities I Have Known." Lorene has a chapter in his book. He admits in the chapter that writing a brief profile of Lorene is almost impossible. "A profile is a small sketch, and one cannot write a same year as the Platform Association convention, 1971, she was one of ten nominees for the Alaskan of the Year Award.

The year after her London trip, Lorene moved The Hat Box and its

1971 - Lorene sits next to Jerry Connor and his 16-year-old daughter "at the big International Platform Association banquet with world speakers and performers."

'small' sketch of Lorene….She has 'started the music' in the lives of countless people. Her record of creative achievement seems beyond the limits of any one individual."

Alaska had noticed her too. That

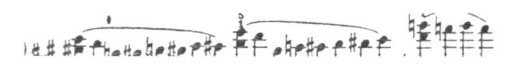

"pretties" to a much larger location on 4th Avenue between E and F streets. Looking back, she is not sure that this was the best business move. "The space was huge. The shop lost some of its charm and intimacy in all that space," she reflects. It was three years later, in 1975, that she moved out of that overly large space to what was then the new University Center, a mall owned by another Kansan, former governor Walter Hickel. Moving in, Lorene called it "the most beautiful mall in Alaska." Her shop seemed to fit in better in this, its last location.

With travel and business filling her time, she still never dropped the thread of civic involvement. Along with her work for the Anchorage Arts Council, she carried out lots of volunteer work in the 1970s, on the boards of organizations such as the Concert Association, Little Theatre, the Anchorage Community Chorus, and the opera. In 1974, the Anchorage Concert Association elected its founder, Lorene, president of the board for its Silver Anniversary year. From 1978 to 1979, she served as Southcentral Alaska campaign director for the March of Dimes.

Family kept her busy as well. Her home was often full of her daughters' families, their children and their husbands. By now there were six grandchildren — Carol Anne's three daughters and one son, (Kelly Anne, Diane Lee, Romney Patricia, and Ed Harrison), and Pegge's two sons (Eric Harrison and Earl Frederick). Lorene's sister, Nina, then in her 80s, flew north to spend the month of June with Lorene in 1972.

Keeping in touch, corresponding with both new and old friends, was also a continuing chord in her life. Lorene was delighted when, in 1971, she received a handwritten note from a woman who had also spent childhood years in Sterling, Kansas. She had been prompted to write by an article she had read about a Lorene Harrison in *GRIT Magazine*, a Sunday supplement magazine appearing in several national newspapers, a Chicago paper, in this instance. Could this be the Lorene from the Cuthbertson family she had known in Sterling, the writer, a Mrs. S.L. Walker, wanted to know? She wrote:

Dear Mrs. Harrison,
When I started to read the article about you in "GRIT Magazine" – Sterling, Kansas caught my eye. (I lived there several years when a child.) As I read on, I thought it has to be Lorene Cuthbertson – Nina's younger sister who was in my sister Lenora Elliott's class in Sterling High School. This Lorene played the piano very well.

We attended the U.P. Church.

Because we were poor and most of us had the flu during that first bad epidemic, lovely Nina asked my mother to let her take me to her family's home. I slept upstairs.

One day when 'you' were playing the piano, I asked Nina to ask you to play a number for me, "The Missouri Waltz." You did…. Your parents were nice to me, also your grandparents who were there at the time. Your grandfather gave me some dried apples. Your father operated a pop factory as I remember.

I was so impressed with your lovely home and good food.

I probably stayed a week. I was bought a pair of brown sandals.

"This is Jeannie Willis who 'brushes up' my hair every day, does my laundry, and generally helps me with numerous housekeeping things. Because of four small strokes, I have lost use of my left hand and leg and Jeannie pinch hits for me."

I suppose the reason I'm writing you is because we thought your family was so nice, and I just felt I would like to know if you are the Lorene of that family.

Just to please me… would you drop us a line? Your career has been remarkable. I, Viola, am 62. Lenora, my only sister living, is 68.
    Respectfully,
    Mrs. S. L. Walker

Of course, Lorene responded shortly after receiving the letter, telling Viola Walker, "I am, indeed, the Lorene Cuthbertson Harrison who was reared in Sterling, Kansas – and proud of it. The letter from you, as a result of the story in *GRIT*, is a real human interest story!"

Lorene's letter continues:
I have had such a very wonderful life, and am 'still going strong' at age 66. The strong Christian background from my own family, from the Sterling community and college, and from my Camp Fire guardian and group, are largely responsible for the attitudes toward life and living which I have, and have been able to pass on in some part to others. The heredity of the Cuthbertsons has given us three children unending vitality. My sister Nina (15 years older than I) is about the most won-

Lorene Harrison

derful person in the world; and my brother Will (still a practicing chiropractor and 21 years older than I) looks forward to each day as another to help those who need him!

I have been alone now nearly ten years, and I am so grateful that I have had consuming interests. You can't believe how many honors I have received – and for doing just what I have enjoyed doing! I dearly love Alaska, and can only believe that a kind Creator sent me to the right place at the right time. I have two wonderful daughters, both so happily married – who between them have given me six grandchildren. I can hardly believe I'm old enough for that!!!

I am going to send your letter on to Nina (Wyatt), now living in the Presbyterian Manor in Sterling. I stop in the old home town about every second year as I fly between Anchorage and New York. Nina will enjoy your letter immensely. Her memory is keen and fresh and alert.

Thank you so much for your interesting letter.
        Sincerely,
        Lorene

Lorene — still fresh and keen and alert, herself — would tell you that in 1978, she "retired" when she finally sold The Hat Box that December, by then known simply as "Lorene's."

"Pat Franks who 'does' my hair every Saturday at the Pioneers' Home."

Anyone who knows her would scoff at that word, "retired." Like a too big floppy hat, it doesn't fit. Lorene would tell you too that the era of big hats, or any hats, had dwindled. "In the 1960s, hats were a big deal. People wouldn't go out the door without a hat – both men and women. Big hair, women's bouffant styles, came into fashion in the 1970s and generally wiped out hats," she comments. Lorene notes that she had never been one to wear big broad-brimmed hats. "At my height, five feet four inches, I wouldn't have carried them well."

She adds that when she went to her trademark hair style, her beautiful white hair, curled and towering tall and softly over her head, she couldn't wear hats. "That's been almost 20 years now." For all those years she has had the same hair stylist, Pat Franks, who now comes to the Pioneers' Home each Saturday to do Lorene's hair. "It's wonderful to still have her," Lorene comments. "She always does my hair, nice and neat. I get many compliments. And besides that, she's a real friend!"

Helping Lorene maintain Pat Franks' hairstyling each morning is Jeannie Willis. "She comes in every day but Sunday to do laundry for so many here at the Pioneers' Home," Lorene states, "including mine, as a part-time paid position. But she even comes in on Sunday to straighten up my hair and to make me presentable." Looking attractive, seven days a week, has always been important to Lorene.

Another set of helping hands belongs to Virginia Carter. "She comes every Thursday afternoon as a volunteer here and at other senior facilities," Lorene explains. "She runs all kinds of errands for the residents at the Pioneers' Home, and will take no money for her kindness. She'll say, 'Some day I may be elderly and will need this same kind of help.' I am very grateful to her."

Virginia Carter smiles at an awards ceremony in the Mayor's office, spring of 1999.

Chapter Fifteen
1980s — "Retirement"
"When things get too hard, I take a nap."

Retirement means different things to different people. Some take up napping. Lorene says she has long mastered the art of napping, that it is not something that came to her in her late 70s and retirement. "In difficult moments, rather than becoming too stressed, I could nap at the drop of a hat. I can sleep anytime," she boasts, adding, "When things get too hard, I take a nap. When the kids were young, and I was running from one responsibility to another, I'd just throw myself across the double bed, on my stomach, and go out. Ten minutes and I'd be refreshed. I could get back to going." She was power napping long before it had a name – ahead of her time, as she was in so many other aspects of her life.

This trick came up while Lorene was reflecting on another energy source, her spiritual life. She has always drawn on her faith for strength and energy, while growing up as a Presbyterian in a strong Presbyterian family in Kansas, while directing the Anchorage Presbyterian Church choir for 27 years, and, for a period of a few years in Anchorage, as a member of the Church of Religious Science. "I got sidetracked into that faith. I've always been interested in studying many religions," Lorene comments. And, yes, there is another first in this spiritual history. "The first formal meeting of the Religious Scientists

Lorene takes a group of Religious Science friends "to see the beauties at Alyeska."

Bee Culver, who introduced Lorene to Religious Science - "She was an interior decorator. She helped with the interior design of the Atwood home and the (Marguerite) Johnson home - and stayed with me at my home."

here was held in my third-floor living room back in the 1960s," she relates. "A friend, Bee Culver, from Seattle, introduced me to this religion. She had stayed in my Anchorage home, off and on."

Today, Lorene carries her own version of a strong faith with her on her daily rounds, something developed over the years. Does she use meditation? "I do, in my own way. All through the day, when something good happens, I find myself saying, 'Thank you, Father.' We all have a lot to be thankful for."

During the 1980s, travel took up far more of Lorene's time than any cat napping. Her traveling companion on many of her far-reaching trips was childhood friend, Erma Liska, from the Sterling, Kansas days. Lorene gives a brief background to this friendship of over eight decades. "You remember that Erma, Erma Hildeman then, had lived with my family in Sterling for a year, when she was in the eighth grade, that both her father and mother had died. Her mother died from tuberculosis, called consumption back then. I can't remember the cause of her father's death. My parents took her in while the extended family worked out more permanent arrangements for Erma and her two brothers. Eventually Erma was sent to California to live with relatives there, but we corresponded all through the years and visited when we could. Erma always remembered my parents on special occasions such as anniversaries, she was so grateful to them. She'd often send them flowers, and she made a beautiful quilt for my wedding."

In 1979, Lorene and Erma traveled together to the Caribbean, a trip they would later repeat and go through the Panama Canal, followed in 1980 by a trip to the South Pacific, New Zealand, Australia, New Guinea and islands in between. They journeyed to China in 1982, and in 1983, their travels took them to the east coast during the fall foliage season. In 1984, Lorene went to Austria, Italy, Morocco, Spain, and Portugal with Delores Dash, an Anchorage friend of many years and still Lorene's accountant.

Earlier in the '80s, in 1981, Lorene took off by herself for Scotland, tracing Scottish ancestral roots on her father's side. She has a photo of the family

Lorene and her childhood friend and traveling companion in the 1980s, Erma Liska.

This is Erma and Lorene, on a South Pacific tour. "Her son, Bob, and his wife, Darlene, were in Tahiti attending a convention, and we met them there in 1980."

home there, Habbieauld Farm, in Kilmaurs Parish, Ayrshire, Scotland. It is on the cover of a family history titled "Memories of Ayrshire, Illinois and Kansas by the family of Alexander Cuthbertson, 1813-1860, et al." Alexander is Lorene's grandfa-

"This is the photo my second cousin, Robert Cuthbertson, sent to me from Scotland — so that I could identify him when I got off the plane. But it was taken in much younger days, so I really didn't know what he looked like!"

ther. The intricate history was collected and typed by Lorene's second cousin, a professional genealogist, William C. Cuthbertson, in 1972. Wonderful old family photos — one ancestor after another staring rather grimly straight ahead — fill its pages, complementing over 100 pages of text. The volume adds to the impression that this has long been a family of many fine writers and musicians.

For Lorene, the thrill of this trip came from knowing that her feet were walking over the same concrete flooring as so many of her family members, four generations before her in that old stone family home. To the best of Lorene's knowledge, Cuthbertsons are living there to this day.

In planning her trip to this homeland, Lorene corresponded back and forth with another second cousin, Robert Cuthbertson, whom she had never met. In order to recognize each other at the small country airport outside the seaside village of Ayr, Scotland, they had exchanged photos. "He'd sent me a photo of himself in much younger days, so I really didn't have a clue what he would look like at the time. I'd had a long layover at the London airport, then boarded a small plane to Ayr. I was five hours late getting in, and hoping so much someone would still be at the little airport to meet me. When I got off the plane at 11 p.m., this tall and handsome gentleman came rushing over, took me in his arms and kissed me, smack on the lips. 'Boy, I hope you're Robert,' I told him. I

Lorene's Travel Photos from the 1980s

The mountains rise directly out of the Li River in China. We were on a steamer for several hours.

The famous Sydney Opera House. We spent several hours touring this building.

The very famous Great Wall of China.

One of the diminishing number of panda bears in China.

The Rock of Gibralter.

Mostly Music

Having dinner in China.

Lorene's Travel Photos from the 1980s

Visiting a tribe in New Guinea.

A castle in Ireland.

A friendly Irish waiter helps me get ready for dinner in Ireland.

was startled. 'Yes, and I know that you are Lorene,' he told me. 'You are the only woman on the plane!' He did a wonderful job of taking me around the countryside, telling me the Cuthbertson history and showing me landmarks. We toured a country church yard, with huge old tombstones bearing the family name."

From Scotland, Lorene joined a tour arranged by a travel agency and went on to England and Ireland.

Shortly after this Scotland trip, Lorene sold her home of 30 years on the 10th Avenue Park Strip and moved into a condo on 12th Avenue, the Park Place Condominiums. It was 1982. "It was time," Lorene states simply. "I was 77 and my knees were beginning to give out." Never one to complain, when Lorene begins to list health problems, there is no doubt that they are significant. "My eyes had begun to fail, and my singing voice began to give out. I had given up solo work after I was 60."

"Look on the Sunny Side," words from a popular song, are words that Lorene chooses to live by. She found much to like in her new setting. "I had my own garage, good services, my own deck. I put planters all over it and even got a prize for 'best flowers.'"

Then there are the memories of "wonderful bread, fresh baked," from these condo days. Friends

Charmaine Welling and Lorene in 1993 — Lorene calls her "one of the best bread bakers in America." "Every month I get a little box of six loaves. I cherish them, as I do her for her wonderful long-distance love and caring, and I occasionally send her a check for parcel post for these treasures."

inevitably followed Lorene from her Park Strip home to her condo, stopping by to visit once she was settled there. One of these, Charmaine Welling, began bringing over her fresh baked bread for Lorene when she had guests. "It was so good! I asked her if she would do this for me once in awhile. Well, it's been a long while – many, many years. Charmaine has moved to Utah, but she's kept sending me little loaves of her bread – a much appreciated labor of love."

John Brower, former executive director of the Anchorage Concert Chorus - Lorene comments, "How can I say enough nice things about John? He and his car are always available to me for concerts!"

Long blessed with what she calls "wonderful health," 1982 brought major health issues Lorene's way. "In 1982, I was diagnosed with colon cancer," she states. "It all happened so fast. My regular doctor for about 25 years, Dr. Robert Wilkins, sent me to Dr. William Bowers. Dr. Bowers was suspicious, and did a colonoscopy and some other tests. They came back positive, and surgery followed quickly. Dr. Steven Menaker was my surgeon, and we became personal friends. I told him I had complete confidence in him, and after the surgery I sent him a thank you note, praising what he had done for me. In response, he sent me a lovely bouquet of flowers, a gesture of friendship. I was home from Providence Hospital within five days." Lorene has been cancer-free for 18 years.

Then followed a diagnosis of Crohn's Disease, soon after surgery. A dysfunction of the bowels, Lorene calls it "a big inconvenience, keeping me close to my home." She comments, "It wasn't bad until the mid-1990s. Some people have terrible stomach pains with Crohn's, and I've never had a single pain."

Now it has required a much modified lifestyle, however, and, as Lorene puts it, "heavy doses of Imodium when I get away for very special events, such as occasional musicals." She adds, "Wonderful friends take me, such as Julie Guy, president of the board of the Performing Arts Center, and John Brower, who was executive director of the Concert Chorus."

She handles her Crohn's Disease like she tackles life in general —

problems struck, Lorene received a singular honor. Mayor George Sullivan declared March 19, 1981 "Lorene Harrison Day." This designation had been instigated by the teachers' sorority, Delta Kappa Gamma, in recognition of Lorene's

Julie Guy, a former president of the board of the Performing Arts Center - Lorene calls her "a great friend ever since she came to Anchorage, and one of the most intelllectual women I know!"

directly, head on. When visiting with friends or out and about, she'll simply say, "I'm going to have to make a little trip," and head off to the restroom. "I'm not embarrassed," she says. "It's something we all do. I just do it more."

In 1981, before these major health

over 50 years of cultural and civic contributions to Anchorage. Fortunately for the people who make plaques, not each and every one of Lorene's contributions was engraved. A proclamation, signed by the mayor and sorority president, Mary Flynn, carries a list over 40 contributions long.

On her designated day, the *Anchorage Times* ran a feature tribute. Dated March 19, 1981, it summarizes, "A list of the organizations which have felt the touch of Lorene Harrison would cover just about every one in Anchorage," and proclaims, "If Anchorage didn't have what Lorene Harrison wanted in arts activities, then she simply started them herself. That's been the philosophy of this local leader in the arts world for over 54 years, and Delta Kappa Gamma, an international honorary teachers' society, didn't want Anchorage to forget all that Harrison has done."

The article continues, "Therefore, today is Lorene Harrison Day, a time set aside for everyone from Mayor George Sullivan to each member of the Anchorage Community Chorus to those who enjoyed this week's performance of the Pacific Northwest Ballet to make note of Harrison's contributions to and love of the arts."

Asked on "her day" what she considered her greatest achievement, she decided it would be the founding of the Anchorage Concert Association because "it's still functional 100 percent, full steam ahead." She's quoted in the article as adding, "Since I founded it in 1950, I'm so proud of the way Dr. (Robert) Wilkins has continued with this. We had a completely full house at the dance recital this week (Pacific Northwest Ballet). It's so gratifying to know that you're pleasing so many people, and that's what life is all about, isn't it?"

March 19, 1981 - Mayor George Sullivan declares this date "Lorene Harrison Day." Lorene says about the moment caught in the photo, "Mayor George Sullivan is giving me just the <u>right</u> kind of city honor." She and the mayor are shown here with Mary Flynn, president of Delta Kappa Gamma teachers' sorority, the group which had instigated this honor.

Looking back today, to what she considers her most significant achievements, she would add planting the seeds for the Anchorage Concert Chorus, formerly the Anchorage Community Chorus. "It, too, is still full steam ahead," she states.

Lorene may have stepped aside from her active leadership roles by the 1980s, but the community certainly didn't forget her. Bob Atwood put it this way, in a tribute to Lorene and a kind of "state of the arts" summary published in his "Between Us" column in the *Anchorage Times*. The column is dated February 4, 1979. First he remembered how, in the days well before computers, beginning around the 1930s, the tracking of community arts activities fell to the Community Calendar created by the *Anchorage Times*. (In 1979, it was being resurrected as a community service by the Anchorage Chamber of Commerce.) He calls the original calendar "a kind of do-it-yourself project" kept in an oversized diary book on the front counter in the *Times* front office. "Local groups planning bake sales, pancake breakfasts, spring luncheons or other social, civic or charitable events made a note of their plans in that book. Mrs. Tafton even wrote in the book the dates for the concerts of her piano students." (As an aside, Lorene comments, "My daughter, Pegge, was one of her students, as well as Marilyn Atwood.")

The *Times* column continues, "Many, if not most, of the cultural events that were recorded in that Community Calendar were in the handwriting of Lorene Harrison. She was the prime mover in bringing to Anchorage what were considered real highbrow arts." Bringing his comments up to the current date, 1979, Atwood added, "Since retiring from active musical leadership, television and business, Lorene's role has been different. Something like the Queen Mother of the arts. Elvera Voth took over as artistic director of the civic opera. Dewey Ehling became conductor of the community chorus. Dr. Robert Wilkins is the volunteer manager of the Concert Association. Maurice Dubonnet conducts the symphony orchestra. Carol Derfner manages the arts council. (About two years after this column was written, Ira Perman would become the paid executive director of the Concert Association.)

"It must take a dozen or more to carry on the programs and organizations left in the wake of Lorene's path through history."

Perhaps Lorene was out of the limelight of busy participation, but certainly not left in the shadows. In 1981, a few months after her Lorene Harrison Day tribute, she was honored at a convention of the International Festivals and Northwest Festivals Association, held in Anchorage that fall. Lorene explains, "Each year an award would be given to someone in the host city for their distinguished service to their community and society. It was a dinner, and I hadn't planned to go. Farrel Vail, who was head of all the Miss Alaska pageants through the 1960s, called, asking if I would go to the dinner with her mother, that she needed company. Farrel and my daughter Pegge had been best friends in school here. Of course, I said 'yes.' Well, I didn't even know about the award, but as a list of the contributions of the person to be recognized was being read at the dinner, I slowly realized, 'Hey, that's me!' I was the very surprised recipient!"

About two weeks later, on October 18, 1981, the *Anchorage Daily News* carried a story about the event. The headline reads, "Lorene Harrison honored at joint festivals convention," and states, "The honoree was surprised, but she shouldn't have been. Lorene Harrison, who received the Community Service award from two festivals on October 2, has been honored many times in the past for her long and valued service to Anchorage civic and cultural activities." Over 250 leaders in the production of celebrations had been in town for the IFA/

Farrel Vail and her husband Bill in Lorene's Park Strip home, where they were married. Lorene explains, "Farrel did all the planning and organizing through the 1960s for the local Miss Alaska pageants, on through the Miss America pageants - an enormous job - well done!"

NFA convention, hosted that year by Fur Rendezvous.

The next year, on September 23, 1982, Lorene was honored by her alma mater, Sterling (Kansas) High School and its National Honor Society. "It's interesting that this honor came on the 60th anniversary of my high school graduation," Lorene states. "It meant so much to me, that at age 77, I made the trip back to Sterling to receive it in person. It was called the 'Black Bear Award.' The beautiful plaque says it is given to recognize a Sterling High alumnus for inspirational achievements in service and leadership."

Back in 1978, Lorene had been given the Distinguished Service award from Sterling College, only the third person in the 100-year history of the college to receive it. She had traveled back to receive this also, at the college graduation ceremonies.

Toward the end of the '80s, as the city's new performing arts center was being dedicated and its lobbies and three theaters named, Lorene found herself back in the spotlight of community attention. What to name the center and the individual areas within it? Lorene's name was put forth for the entire complex. The *Anchorage Daily News* reported on June

"I am attending the 60th anniversary of my high school graduation in Sterling, Kansas. I was honored for inspirational achievements in service and leadership - and felt so honored, I made the trip back to receive the award in person."

23, 1988, that a meeting to consider names had been held the day before. "Most of the 20 people who attended preferred to name the center for Lorene Harrison," the reporter states, "who came to Anchorage as a public school music teacher in 1928 and evidently has founded, directed, or served on practically every arts group in town since then." Mention is made of the fact that Larry Beck was in attendance, supporting the Harrison name. "Larry Beck, a seasonal entertainer who puts on an Alaskana show mainly for tourists, said naming the center for Harrison would improve its public profile. 'This lady is head and shoulders above everybody else in what she's done,' he said."

History tells us that the suggestion was ultimately rejected, and today Lorene tends to shrug it off. "Eventually there was so much controversy surrounding almost everything about the center – not just its naming, but the design of the whole building, even the carpeting and the restroom decorations, that I found it just as well not to be at the center of it," she muses.

On September 6, 1988, the decision fell to the Anchorage Assembly,

Here is Lorene receiving the Distinguished Service Award from Sterling College in 1978 — only the third person in the 100 year history of the college to receive this award.

voting to name the center the Alaska Center for the Performing Arts. A *Daily News* article dated September 8, 1988 comments, "The assembly yielded to the wishes of directors and executives of Alaska Center for the Performing Arts Inc., the nonprofit corporation created by the city to operate the center. They rejected a suggestion to name the center for Lorene Harrison, a champion of the arts since she arrived in Anchorage in 1928...."

To this day, Lorene does not know who first suggested her name for the center. If a lobby says "Come on in," then a very appropriate part of the Performing Arts Center was to be named for Lorene, the three-stories high main lobby stretching between Fifth and Sixth avenues and facing Town Square. It is located outside the largest of the three theaters, now called the Atwood Theater for Evangeline Atwood. It was the Anchorage Concert Association that raised the funds, $55,000, to see that Lorene's name was placed on the lobby.

All controversy aside, Lorene delights in remembering conducting the *Alaska Flag Song* from "her" balcony at the gala opening of the

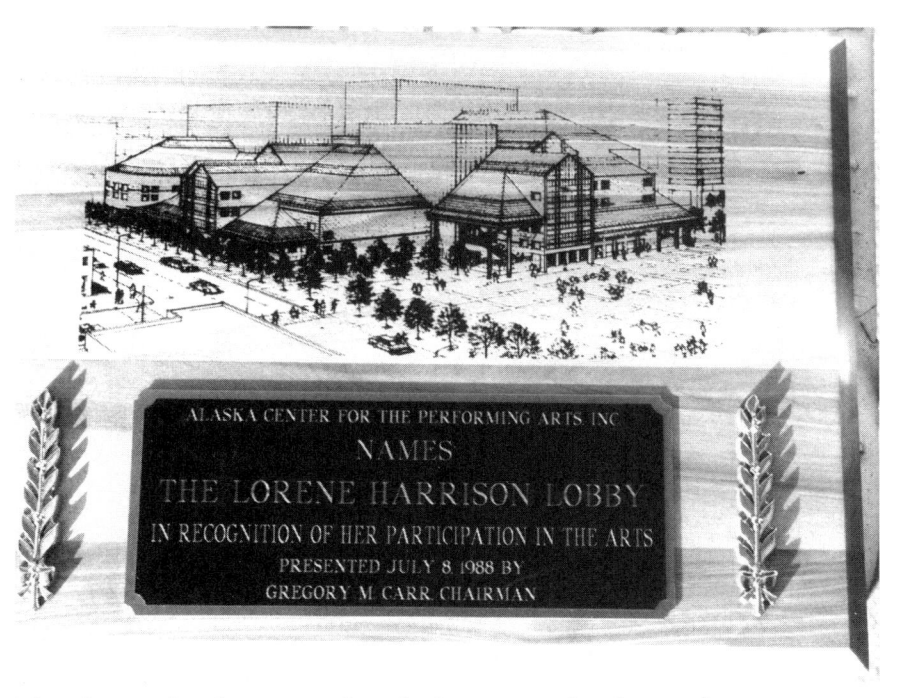

The plaque that hangs in the Alaska Center for the Performing Arts, naming the main lobby for Lorene Harrison in 1988 when the Center opened.

PAC during the weekend of December 16th and 17th that year. "I stood way up on the third floor balcony, by the rail. There were crowds of people standing and sitting below. I conducted the *Flag Song* from there, and everybody joined in singing. It was just wonderful."

Chapter Sixteen
"My Life's Been Full; I Savored Much."

"Night is closing in." That is how Lorene, entering the decade of the 1990s, expressed the fact of her aging. As the decade began, she was already 85, and in her own words, "far more friends have 'gone on' than remain."

Still, as the decade of the '90s draws to a close, the phone rings often, bringing news of friendships far and near, friendships still very much alive. Still, Lorene maintains her gracious nature, seeking out life's little joys, delighting in sharing in many ways with others, often sharing her stories. "Prepare to laugh," she'll say. "Here's a little story." Then she'll come out with an anecdote or joke from long ago, often in amazing detail, bringing on her own merriment. Her life is full of happy notes, mixed in with some pain. She chooses to remember the joy.

Still, her hair is beautifully done, arranged carefully each day into her trademark tall white curls. She dresses with equal care and attention, often in soft print blouses, matched to her slacks, with earrings and a pretty necklace in coordinating colors. There is no slouch in her. One can't imagine that there ever was. The servers in the Pioneers' Home dining room are often heard commenting, "Oh, Lorene. You look beautiful."

"Come in," she'll sing in a cheerful,

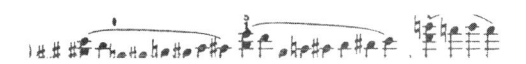

Mostly Music

Lorene was named "Alaskan of the Year" in 1992. "I'm holding my plaque, just after receiving it - very proudly!"

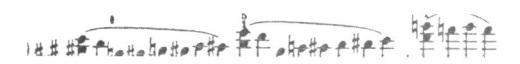

chipper voice in answer to any knock at her door.

Still, Lorene has great affection for her community, for Anchorage. "I can't imagine living anywhere else," she'll say. "It's such a beautiful place, just full of talent. I knew right away this was the place where I wanted to live, right away. It's always been that way."

The community continues to return that praise and affection. She's been here so long and done so much that she is often honored at the 25th or 50th anniversaries of various organizations, many of them looking to her as their founder. As the decade began, the First Presbyterian Church called her back to be the guest conductor for the 75th anniversary celebration of its founding. The year was 1915, just 13 years before Lorene arrived in town. On November 23, 1990, a reflective article was printed in the *Anchorage Daily News*, looking back on all that Lorene had done for that church choir and so many other Anchorage organizations. "Musical Pioneer Performs Encore," its headline reads, and describes the anniversary performance on Sunday, November 17 that year. "Under her guidance for two services last Sunday were some of her old

Excited by the prestigious award, given out since 1967 to one distinguished Alaskan each year, grandson Ed Dodd, who owned an Anchorage Texaco station, made a proud public announcement. ("Grandma Hat" had been a "pet" family nickname for Lorene for many years.)

choir compatriots, people like former newspaper publisher Robert Atwood and soprano Kathryn Chenoweth.

"Chenoweth, who sang for Harrison for the whole 27 years (that Lorene conducted the Presbyterian Choir), says the Harrison she saw Sunday 'was the same old Lorene. She hadn't forgotten a thing.' "Says Harrison: 'It was like going back home.'"

The article goes on to cite many of Lorene's civic contributions, then adds, "But arts, especially musical arts, have been the cornerstone of her life. She organized or helped organize such groups as the Anchorage Concert Association and the Anchorage Community Chorus (now called the Anchorage Concert Chorus) and served on the boards of many others. Concert Association executive director Ira Perman calls her 'the founding mother of the arts in Anchorage . . . one of our great pioneers.'

"Harrison chalks it up to love. 'I've done so many things with music,

Lorene gathered in 1994 with others who had received the Alaskan of the Year award. Left to right, and the year they received the award: Walter Hickel (1969), George Sullivan (1982), Larry Carr (1984), Dr. William Wood (1985), Bill Tobin (1988), Frank Reed Sr. (1990), Lorene (1992), Mrs. Jack M. (Kay) Linton (1993), Bill Allen (1994), Jay Hammond (1995), Perry Green (1996). photo by Rob Stapleton

and I've loved them all,' she says. 'That's why I'm still young at 85.'"

In the same feature, Elvera Voth, then conductor of the Alaska Chamber Singers and artistic director of the Alaska Festival of Music, commented on the enthusiasm Lorene sparked in others from the time she first arrived back in 1928, adding, "The performing arts were looking for a visionary and they found one in Lorene."

In 1992 it was not just Anchorage paying tribute to Lorene, but the State of Alaska. She received the honor of Alaskan of the Year. Thrilled with the honor, Lorene wrote of it in her annual Christmas letter to family and friends that year. (These "letters" are legend, really mini books, full of news and stories and family photos.) She first gives some background to the award. "Since 1967, a very prestigious award has been given each year to one person in Alaska, the title being 'ALASKAN OF THE YEAR.' Anyone in the state may make a nomination by submitting supportive information showing 'outstanding contributions by a living Alaskan over the years, which have significantly affected the character and development of

Former Alaska Governor, Steve Cowper, presenting Lorene with a State of Alaska plaque for enriching Alaska with music and culture.

Tony Knowles, Governor of Alaska, visiting Lorene at the Pioneer's Home in 1998 — "I've known him for 30 years. On the photo he wrote, 'Lorene, Great to see you. Thanks for your service to Alaska.'"

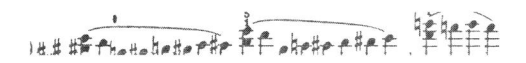

the 49th state.' The individual is selected by a statewide electorate composed of 60 people geographically distributed according to legislative apportionment, the Alaskan of the Year Board, and recipients of the Alaskan of the Year Award who still reside in Alaska.'"

"One of the Men at My Table" - Walter Williams.

Her Christmas "booklet" then goes on to describe her own recognition. "Well, it turns out that I was one of five finalists. They do not disclose who submitted your name. Two of the men were millionaire philanthropists, so I went to the banquet expecting to applaud one of them. I was truly stunned when it was announced that 'Lorene Harrison is the 1992 ALASKAN OF THE YEAR.' Bob Atwood, the very first recipient, gave my story….The past recipients have been some of our governors, U.S. Alaska Senators, pioneer aviators, early bankers, newspaper editors, university presidents, etc. Very good company! Thus, you will see my picture holding the beautiful plaque in these pages."

The *Daily News*, March 31, 1992, told the story under the headline "Harrison Joins State's Elite – City's 'Mother of the Arts' Chosen Alaskan of the Year."

Along with this happy and prestigious news, Lorene's same Christmas letter of 1992 brought news of a family tragedy. Lorene's grandson Earl, Pegge and Joe Vielbig's son, died suddenly at age 33, a drowning accident which occurred during his daily swim at an athletic club near his California home. He left his wife, Sharon, and their baby son, four-month-old Steven. Lorene says, "He was a loving and beloved member of our family. He will be missed forever."

In the fall of 1994, "at Halloween,"

Lorene remembers, she moved into the Anchorage Pioneers' Home on West 11th Avenue downtown, leaving her condo. "It was the right thing to do," Lorene states. "The Crohn's disease played a large part in my decision." She faces her move to her room there with her usual acceptance of life's passages. "I've enjoyed the Pioneers' Home, getting things organized here — in some kind of order for my children."

She pauses, looking around her room full of memorabilia, her "stuff" she calls it, and there is a great deal of it in a small space, mostly scrapbooks in boxes and autographed photos of the people who have moved through her life. "I spend more time in my room. I'm really gregarious — I suppose I'm surprised at the amount of time I spend here in my room." She adds, "Some may resent being here. I feel it was right to come here. I was getting older, my knees are getting bad, I have the Crohn's to deal with. I needed the security here, the help in the ordinary things of life." She waves her hands, as if dismissing any negatives. "I'm comfortable here."

Then she adds with candor, "I could have made it much more uncomfortable. I chose not to. No, it's not ideal. No, I wouldn't call it absolutely great. But it's right for me now. In so much of life we have a choice of our attitude."

Ed and Aenid Callihan — two of Lorene's "best friends" at the Pioneers' Home, and before.

Not surprisingly, she has collected a group of friends in this setting. "Some I knew before, like Rica Swanson Niemi and her husband, Frank, and some members of my Presbyterian choir. Most I had not known before.

Lots of us look out for each other – in all kinds of little ways." Watch and you'll see them walking each other back to the door of their rooms, getting the mail or bringing the newspaper for each other, tucking in a napkin for a friend at the dinner table, holding the elevator door open for each other.

Another "Man at My Table" — Vince Doran.

Lorene describes in her own words the simple touches of kindness brought to her life at the Pioneers' Home by what she calls "the men at my table," beginning at her very first day as a resident in the Home.

"When an attendant at the Pioneers' Home was starting to seat me for my first meal in the dining room there, about five years ago, Walter Williams saw me, and asked if I could sit at a vacant place at his table. We knew each other slightly, socially – for perhaps 50 years or more. He became a sort of caretaker for me. I eat only fruit and toast for breakfast, and my rising hour is 8 a.m. Breakfast in the dining room is at 7 a.m.! When there was something special that Walter thought I would like (bran muffins), he would bring a couple of them to my door and slip a napkin under the door of my room to let me know to 'open up' — my food was there. Then for lunch and dinner he would knock at my door and say, 'Bring your key and come and we'll both go up to eat.' For over two years he saw that I was well cared for. Walter died of stomach cancer, and I've missed his many thoughtful kindnesses.

"Then there was Ed Callihan and his wife Aenid. For nearly 20 years, I had known them, mostly through music organizations and concerts. They had moved into the Pioneers' Home several months before I did, because of Aenid's failing health. She was my best friend here. One December they left to get medical help Outside, and she died suddenly. When Ed returned, I asked him if he would like to sit at my table – with Louis Roger who had been at the same table with Walter and me – so for most of a year he occupied Walter's chair, and walked me to my room after meals, and took very good care of me. But Ed decided to move to a lovely retirement home in Lacey, Washington, to be closer to his two married daughters. We talk by phone perhaps once a month, and he came back to see his many Anchorage friends this past June. We miss him.

"Occupying the room on the floor next to Louis Roger is Vince Doran, a World War II pilot who flew a B17 over Germany when stationed in England. When he returned from the war, he and his wife and four teenaged children moved to Anchorage. His wife, to whom he was very devoted, died less than two years ago, and he then moved into the Pioneers' Home.

Louis suggested we invite him to sit at our table – in the chair Walter and Ed had used. It was a fine day for me when he accepted. He still works part-time, so only on Saturday

Louis Roger — yet another man "Man at My Table."

and Sunday is he with us at the noon meal. My problems have elevated, with very arthritic knees. Vince helps me slowly to my room. He is very thoughtful and does many little things for me. He is a scholar and a very kind and good friend.

Mostly Music

"Through the years that I have been at the Pioneers' Home, Louis Roger holds seat #1 at table #3. He always sees that I have a napkin, two glasses of ice water – but there are to be helpful!" Lorene adds, "Now you know why mealtime is really 'happy hour' for me!"

In 1995, Lorene had sold her car,

Some of the many "Hats Off to Lorene" - a celebration of her 90th birthday, and a fundraiser for the American Cancer Society - "As a cancer survivor myself, the entire celebration had such a special meaning." Over $14,000 was raised from the sale of hats at the benefit, "mostly my own personal hats," causing Lorene to quip, "Maybe I'll have to go back into business!"

several other ladies for whom he does little kindnesses – pushing their wheel chairs up to the table, getting them salad and dessert from the tray table, pushing the elevator button, or doing anything else just shortly after moving into the Pioneers' Home. She'd been driving until she turned 90, and had always loved to drive. Obviously she's always delighted in going places, and would have learned to fly if time had allowed. "I just never had the time to learn to do that. I could have flown up to my cabin and all over the state. But I've flown in lots of other ways," she laughs. "A car by its nature represents independence," Lorene adds. "Selling it was another life passage. But I haven't missed it nearly as much as I thought I would. Carol Anne and her husband Bob are nearby, and are wonderful at taking me places. And so are many friends."

Friends came out in force to remember Lorene on her 90th birthday. And, to Lorene's great joy, it was not to be a celebration centered on just herself and her 90 years. In keeping with her life's pattern, the celebration wove together many of the continuing threads of Lorene's living –- sharing and fundraising for others, fashions and models, laughter and luncheons, health concerns and history — and, most definitely — hats. The gala party, "Hats Off to Lorene," came two months after she turned 90.

It was an auction of many of the hats Lorene had made, long cherished by people in this town, some still in Lorene's possession, about 50 in all. "Mostly they were my personal hats," Lorene explains. They were sold at a luncheon and fashion show to benefit the American Cancer Society, with the John Robert Powers Finishing School and Modeling Agency, owned by Diane Windsor, as event coordinator and major sponsor. "It was held in the Egan Center on a Saturday — May 6, 1995," Lorene remembers. "About 450 people attended, there were a dozen fashion models, and all 50 hats sold. One hat even went for $450! No hats went for less than $100. I couldn't believe it! When the proceeds were totaled, the benefit had raised $14,000 for the cancer society," Lorene states, beaming. "I used to joke, 'I may have to go back into business!'" Many of the

The invitation to the celebration, featuring Lorene's logo from her very popular business, The Hat Box.

women in attendance that day proudly wore Lorene's Hat Box hats, purchased many years ago.

As a cancer survivor herself, the event held even more meaning for Lorene. Today, on the wall of her room in the Pioneers' Home, Lorene displays a photo collage of the models for the "Hats Off" benefit, wearing many of the stylish hats auctioned that day.

Lorene has kept for herself only two of the thousands of hats that passed through The Hat Box. "One is a cerulean-gray mink hat that matched my fur stole that Jack gave me, and the other is a black feathered hat I especially loved," she says.

The day before the auction, the *Daily News* ran an article about Lorene and the history of her hats. "Hat auction fetes Harrison," its headline reads, and the feature then goes on to tell of Lorene's hats, purses, suits, and dresses to be auctioned. "Over the years Harrison has hung onto many hats, purses and outfits, even through her move in 1982 from a four-bedroom house to a two-bedroom condo. But last October, when it finally came time for yet another move, this one to a single room in the Anchorage Pioneers' Home, she knew what was coming.

Lorene conducted the "Stars Spangled Banner" and the "Alaska Flag Song" when Richard Nixon campaigned in Alaska for the U.S. Presidency. For six years she received one of his beautiful Christmas cards.

'I have to do it,' she said recently. 'I was wondering what I was going to do with all those hats.'

"The idea to sell the hats and help the cancer society came about through a conversation between Harrison's daughter, Carol Anne Dodd, and Emily Larson, who's co-chairing the 'Hats Off to Lorene Harrison' luncheon with Laura

Renner (and her mother, Diane Windsor). Harrison, who survived a bout with colon cancer 12 years ago, found the idea appealing.

"So did Diana Kuhns, the cancer society's executive vice president, who is grateful for Harrison's long-time support of the cancer society. And she thinks the hats are quite wonderful.

"'This is such an opportune time, with fashion trends looking towards hats again,' she said. 'It's an opportunity to mix the old with the new – to remember what Anchorage was like years ago.'

"Now that she's wrestling with Crohn's disease, a debilitating intestinal ailment, Harrison figures the Pioneers' Home is right for her. 'It's what I need now. I don't have to do anything myself, practically.'

"Her body may give her trouble, but her brain doesn't skip a beat. She remembers details – what a certain hat was made of, who designed it. A few weeks ago, as volunteers unpacked the hats and other pieces in the cancer office, Harrison had stories for most of them.

"'I went to Paris to buy that one,' she said of a small straw hat with a broad blue ribbon around the rim.

"As the committee examined the purses, they found themselves following Harrison spoor. A pewter-beaded evening bag still held half an orchestra concert ticket from May 21, 1967. Another disgorged the remains of a lipstick. A

Two Kansas girls who came to Alaska to teach school. Neva Eagan, settled in Valdez and married Bill Eagan, who became Alaska's first governor. Lorene and Neva have remained friends all these years.

red fabric purse revealed a mint and four antacid tablets.

"Harrison is pragmatic about getting rid of the auction items, even those with special emotional resonance — like the dress with the dusty-pink beaded bodice she wore to the wedding of her older daughter, Pegge.

"'I can't wear them anyway,' she shrugged. 'They're a part of the past history; it's nice to look back upon, but I don't need them.'"

Delores Dash, on the right, and Lorene traveled together in 1984 to Europe and Moroco. With her in the photo is Fran Suddock, on the left. "These are two of my dear friends at my 92nd birthday lunch at the Pioneers' Home in 1997."

So, Lorene cleared away many of the remnants of her past, bringing smiles and helping others in doing so. But it is not as if all those others have now forgotten her. Every Anchorage Concert Chorus program still declares above its program listings, "Lorene Harrison, Founder." Lorene states with gratitude, "John Brower, executive director of the Concert Chorus, often picks me up for concerts." The Anchorage Concert Association makes many public acknowledgments of Lorene's founding. The Anchorage Opera programs often trace their history to her. When she is in the audience for a performance, the spotlight in the concert hall of the Performing Arts Center is often directed her way before the concert begins, to recognize the woman who began it all, from whom today's music stems.

Lorene's song goes on. It is her desire that her song goes on to the final chapter of her life, to her memorial service — glorious songs of celebration reflective of her joy in the life she has lived and the people who have filled it. As mentioned earlier, Nancy Wellman De Leon, one of the Miss Alaskas now living in Fairbanks, is to sing *The Lord's Prayer*. Paul Rosenthal has agreed to play his arrangement of the *Alaska Flag Song* on the violin. The Anchorage Concert Chorus is to sing the *Hallelujah Chorus* from Handel's *Messiah*. Lorene adds, "Rev. Richard Gay, God willing, will conduct the service. He has been a friend of mine for many years." Then, pausing for added emphasis, she states firmly, "I want it to be joyful. That's a choice I've made."

She'd also request that the poem, *I'm Free*, be read, one reflecting the path of joy she has sought, her walk in faith, and the friendships that made her chosen path so rich for her.

She's even thought through the message for her gravestone. "Lorene Harrison — She was a seeker and a doer. She chose joy."

That reflects the message she would like most to leave with today's youth. "Don't postpone joy."

She has also chosen the final words of this, the story of her life, asking that they be her own, as are the words at its beginning. They come from her holiday greetings booklet of 1997, full of photos of family — her children and their husbands, grandchildren, great grandchildren —all smiling happily at us.

I have been blessed all my life, as a child with my family of loving, wise, Christian parents, sister and brother; then living after marriage in a place I chose to spend the rest of my life; with two adorable little girls who matured into sensitive, caring, talented women, wives, and mothers. Many wonderful friends came into my life. Opportunities opened up in my fields of interest, and many honors have come my way. In almost 93 years of life I have so very much for which to be thankful. You all have had a share in shaping my life. God bless you all!

*With love,
Lorene*

I'm Free

Don't grieve for me, for now I'm free.
I'm following the path God has laid, you see.
I took His hand when I heard His call,
I turned my back and left it all.
I could not stay another day
To laugh, to love, to work, or play.
Tasks left undone must stay that way.
I found the peace at the close of day.
If my parting has left a void,
Then fill it with remembered joys –
A friendship shared, a laugh, a kiss.
Oh yes, these things I too will miss.
Be not burdened with times of sorrow.
I wish you the sunshine of tomorrow.
My life's been full, I savored much.
Good friends, good times, a loved one's touch.
Perhaps my time seemed all too brief.
Don't lengthen it now with undue grief.
Lift up your hearts, and peace to thee –
God wanted me now; He set me free.
    -*anonymous*-

A Life Full of Contributions and Tributes

"I am amazed by all the honors that have come my way," Lorene comments. *"I have had a grand and full life, hopefully giving much back."*

Recognitions of her many contributions have come from many sources. "I have no idea who nominated me for these various honors or inclusions in books. Once I retired, I cancelled all the honorary memberships in these various professional organizations. But the memories — the blessings of being able to make these contributions — are still very much alive."

In Recognition

of · distinguished · service
to · her · community

Anchorage, Alaska

"First Lady of the Year"

°Lorene Harrison°

is presented this

Award · of · Appreciation

by

Beta Sigma Phi

International

Dorothy Chamberlain

March 17, 1951

President

The Alaska Press Club ANNUAL AWARD

LORENE HARRISON

AWARD OF MERIT

Distinguished Woman's TV Program of 1954

April 30, 1955 — Anchorage, Alaska

*Lorene Harrison
Best Dressed Woman Award
Anchorage, Alaska
1966*

Miss Alaska Pageant

DISTINGUISHED SERVICE AWARD

This is to Certify that

Lorene Harrison

contributed immeasurably to the success of

Anchorage Fur Rendezvous

as

Official Chaperone

of the

Miss Alaska

All members of the Miss America Family and Greater Anchorage, Inc., join in expressing their sincere gratitude to you and your committee for your outstanding contribution to our

Scholarship Program

Lorene Harrison
Founder
Anchorage Community Chorus

Alaska 49'er

LORENE HARRISON

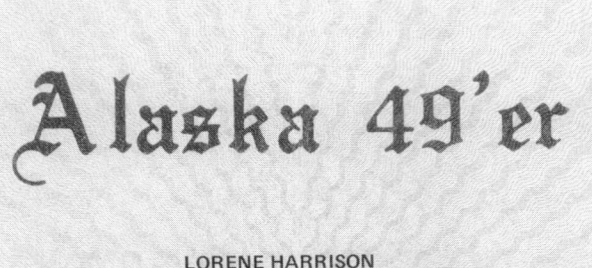

IS HEREBY NAMED AN ALASKA 49'ER

IN THE YEAR OF OUR LORD

1970

IN RECOGNITION OF OUTSTANDING AND
DISTINGUISHED CONTRIBUTION TO THE

State of Alaska

PRESIDENT

CHAIRMAN, BOARD OF GOVERNORS

The Alaska Press Club

THE TWO THOUSAND WOMEN OF ACHIEVEMENT

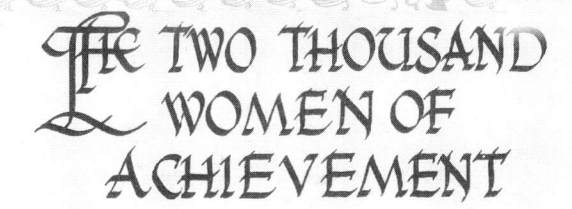

This Diploma is awarded to
Ann Lorene Harrison

for DISTINGUISHED ACHIEVEMENT
and is the subject of commendation in
THE TWO THOUSAND WOMEN OF ACHIEVEMENT 1971

Chairman of the Board

London England

11th August 1971

B J Kirby
Registrar.

The World Who's Who of Women

This Diploma is awarded to

Anne Lorene Harrison

For Distinguished Achievement and is the subject of Commendation in

THE WORLD WHO'S WHO OF WOMEN

April 1973
Cambridge
England

Chairman of the Board

Andrea Hanfman
Registrar

1978
STERLING COLLEGE
DISTINGUISHED SERVICE AWARD
LORENE -CUTHBERTSON- HARRISON
CLASS OF 1928

COMMUNITY SERVICE AWARD
1981
LORENE HARRISON

Presented by Alpha Chapter, Delta Kappa Gamma

to

LORENE CUTHBERTSON HARRISON

In APPRECIATION of and RECOGNITION for Over FIFTY (50) YEARS of

OUTSTANDING SERVICE to the ANCHORAGE COMMUNITY

Educator
Soroptimist
Women's Editor
Business Woman
Pioneers of Alaska
Anchorage Civic Opera
Radio-TV Commentator
Church Music Director
Miss Alaska Chaperone
Musical Extravaganzas
Anchorage Arts Council
Beta Sigma Phi Sorority
First Lady of Anchorage
Greater Anchorage, Inc.
Alaska Festival of Music
Anchorage Little Theatre
Cook Inlet Historical Society
Delta Kappa Gamma Sorority
Anchorage Welcoming Hostess
Alaska World Affairs Council
Anchorage Community Chorus
Anchorage Community Theatre
Anchorage Concert Association
Anchorage Symphony Association
Listed in Numerous Biographies
Anchorage Centennial Commission
Anchorage Chamber of Commerce
International Platform Association
Men's and Women's Civic Glee Clubs
Anchorage Mental Health Association
Metropolitan Opera National Council
Daughters of the American Revolution
Nominated to the Alaskan of the Year Award
Alaska Territorial Golden Rule Mother of the Year

I hereby PROCLAIM that MARCH 19, 1981 be "Lorene Cuthbertson Harrison Day."

_____
President, Delta Kappa Gamma

_____
George M. Sullivan, MAYOR
Anchorage, Alaska

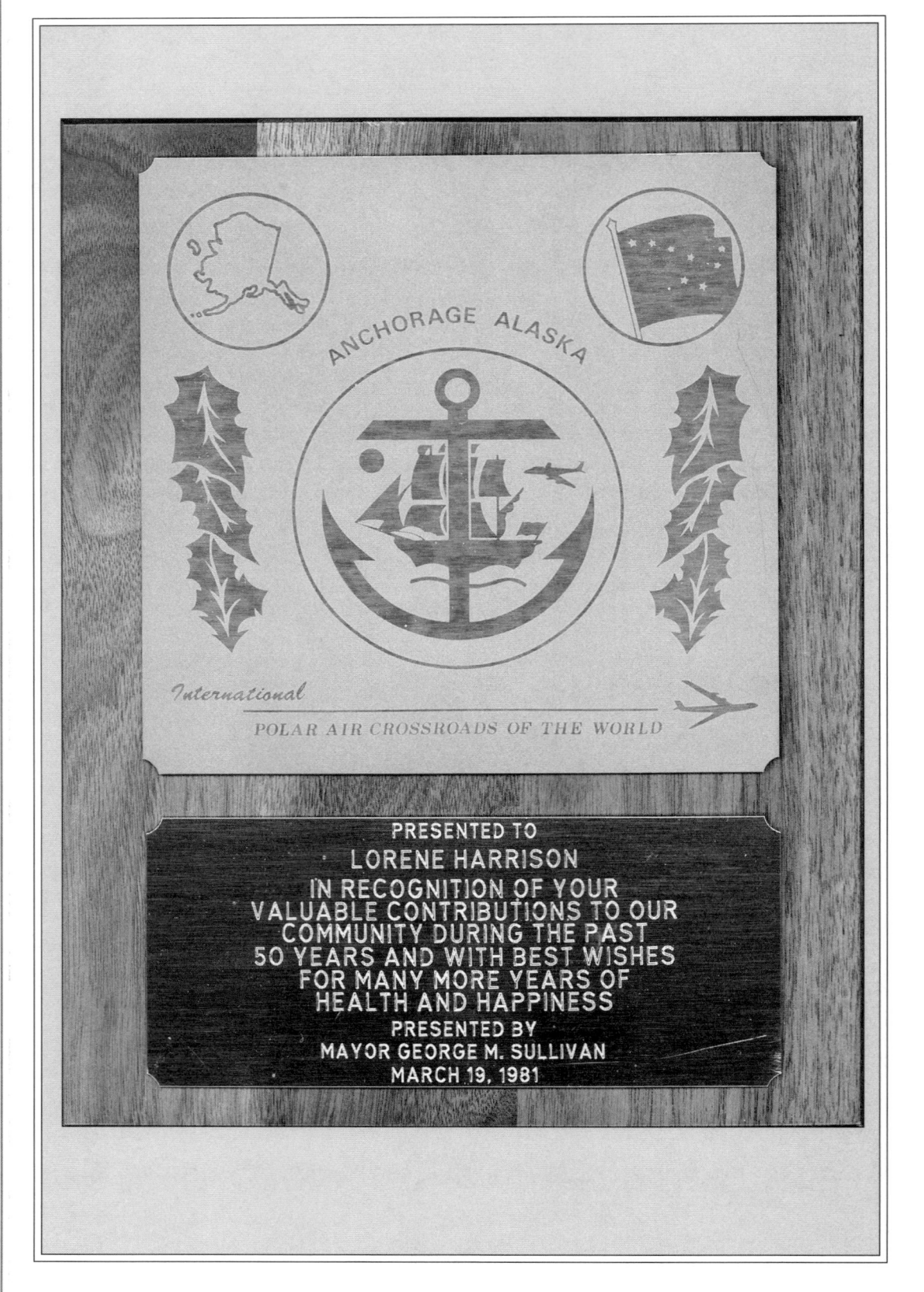

PRESENTED TO
LORENE HARRISON
IN RECOGNITION OF YOUR
VALUABLE CONTRIBUTIONS TO OUR
COMMUNITY DURING THE PAST
50 YEARS AND WITH BEST WISHES
FOR MANY MORE YEARS OF
HEALTH AND HAPPINESS
PRESENTED BY
MAYOR GEORGE M. SULLIVAN
MARCH 19, 1981

State of Alaska

THE LEGISLATURE

HONORING - LORENE HARRISON

The Twelfth Alaska Legislature salutes a noted Alaskan and highly regarded Anchorage civic leader, Lorene Harrison, recently honored by the Municipality of Anchorage through proclamation by Mayor George Sullivan.

For more than 54 years Lorene has contributed her energy and enthusiasm to the creation of a significant number of cultural organizations and events. Perhaps best known of these is the Anchorage Concert Association. Under her leadership, the Anchorage Community Chorus was formed in 1946, and the Concert Association in 1950. She has also devoted a great deal of time to the Anchorage Community Theatre, Anchorage Symphony Orchestra and the Anchorage Civic Opera Association.

Chosen First Lady of Anchorage in 1951, Lorene has traveled extensively, is listed in several national registries and has been honored in the past as one of Alaska's outstanding citizens.

We congratulate and commend the outstanding efforts of this energetic, vivacious and active Alaskan, and extend to her our gratitude for the many contributions she has made to our State.

SPEAKER OF THE HOUSE PRESIDENT OF THE SENATE

Date: April 10, 1981

Requested by: Representative Hayes, Halford, Montgomery and Abood, and Senators Bradley, Sturgulewski, Kelly and Fischer

THIS
1982 "BLACK BEAR AWARD"
IS PRESENTED TO

LORENE HARRISON

BY THE
STERLING HIGH SCHOOL
NATIONAL HONOR SOCIETY

THIS AWARD IS PRESENTED TO A
S.H.S. ALUMNUS SELECTED BY
THE STUDENTS AS DEMONSTRATING
INSPIRATIONAL ACHIEVEMENTS
IN SERVICE AND LEADERSHIP

Lorene C. Harrison

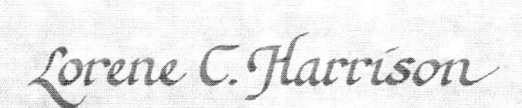

has been inducted this day into
THE AMERICAN BIOGRAPHICAL INSTITUTE's

DIRECTORY OF DISTINGUISHED AMERICANS
HALL OF FAME

for

Outstanding Community Activism

officiated by the
Governing Board of Editors of The American Biographical Institute

permanently documented in the
ABI Library and Archives

and
scheduled for exclusive recognition in
the third and all subsequent editions of the
Directory of Distinguished Americans

Date: *March 16, 1985*

Governing Board of Editors:

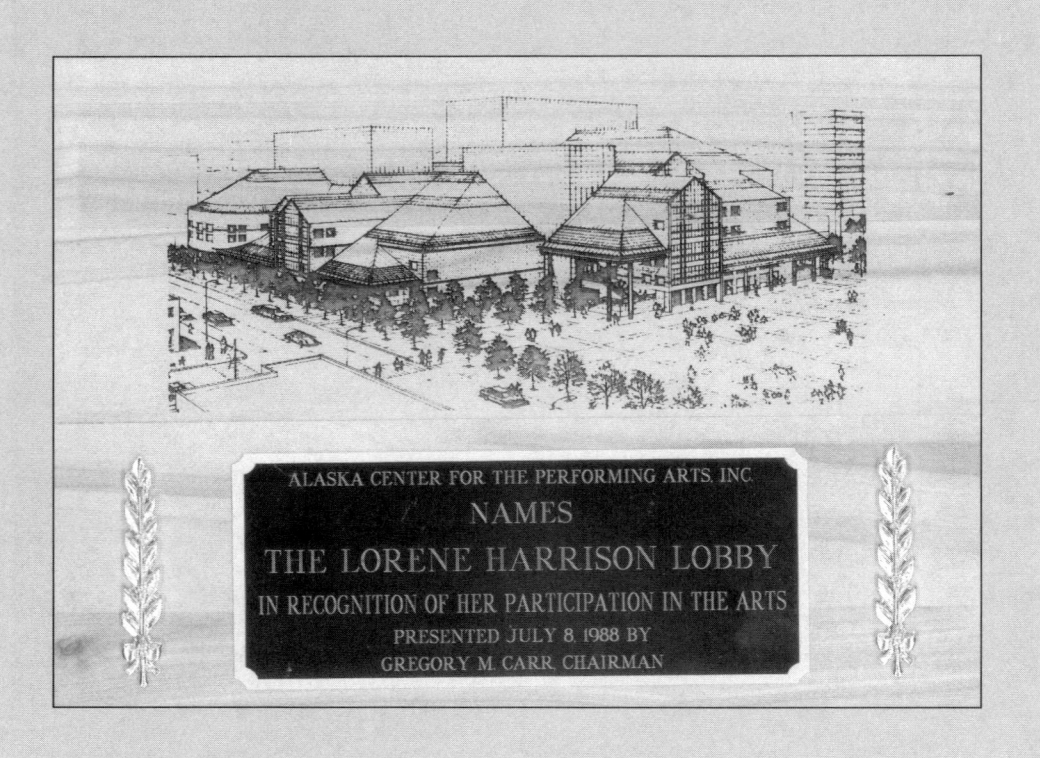

In performing arts programming development,
for outstanding contributions which have
increased the artistic excellence of Alaska,
this *Governor's Award* for the arts
is hereby presented to
Lorene Harrison
April 25, 1987

GOVERNOR OF ALASKA

CHAIRMAN, ALASKA STATE COUNCIL ON THE ARTS

ALASKA CENTER FOR THE PERFORMING ARTS, INC.
NAMES
THE LORENE HARRISON LOBBY
IN RECOGNITION OF HER PARTICIPATION IN THE ARTS
PRESENTED JULY 8, 1988 BY
GREGORY M. CARR, CHAIRMAN

**LORENE HARRISON
WOMAN OF DISTINCTION
MAY 25, 1989**

ALASKAN OF THE YEAR

1992

LORENE HARRISON

The Anchorage Concert Chorus
proudly presents this tribute
to
LORENE HARRISON
Founder of the Anchorage Community Chorus
on this 50th anniversary

Presented on November 1, 1996
Fourth Avenue Theatre
Celebrating Fifty Years of Song
1947 – 1997

This is to certify that

Lorene C. Harrison

has been selected for inclusion in
**The Directory of Distinguished Americans
Third Edition**
for

Fifty Years of Community Service

Presented by
The American Biographical Institute

Official Authorization
Registrars of Awards

Appendix
Lorene Cuthbertson Harrison is listed in the following books.
I never knew who presented my name for inclusion in the following books.

1958   First edition of WHO'S WHO OF AMERICAN WOMEN

1964   DICTIONARY OF INTERNATIONAL BIOGRAPHY (published in London)

1969   FIVE HUNDRED FIRST FAMILIES OF AMERICA by DuBin

1970   ROYAL BLUE BOOK (published in London)

1972   PERSONALITIES OF THE WEST AND MIDWEST

1969   COMMUNITY LEADERS OF AMERICA

1969   FOREMOST WOMEN IN COMMUNICATIONS

1969   First edition of THE 2000 WOMEN OF ACHIEVEMENT IN THE ENGLISH SPEAKING WORLD

1969   NATIONAL REGISTER OF PROMINENT AMERICANS

1970   NATIONAL SOCIAL REGISTER

1970   INTERCONTINENTAL BIOGRAPHICAL ASSOCIATION

1970   Selected by Alaska Press Club to permanent ALASKA HALL OF FAME

1972   First issue of CREATIVE AND SUCCESSFUL PERSONALITIES (2000 persons selected from 5000 recommendations)

1972   HEREDITARY REGISTER OF THE UNITED STATES OF AMERICA

1973   THE WORLD WHO'S WHO OF WOMEN

1973   INTERNATIONAL WHO'S WHO IN COMMUNITY SERVICE

1973   COMMUNITY LEADERS AND NOTEWORTHY AMERICANS

1976   NOTABLE AMERICANS OF THE BICENTENNIAL ERA

Index

A

AAC 181
Abernethy, Bob 75
Above All, A Hat 4
Afield, Walter 161, 162,
.... 211, 213, 214
Alaska Blue Book 153
Alaska Center for the Performing Arts
.... 203
Alaska Chamber Singers 209
Alaska Festival of Music 145, 209
Alaska Flag Song 85, 86, 204, 218
Alaska Methodist University 161
Alaska Music Trail 115, 118,
.... 121, 123
Alaska Pacific University 161
Alaska Press Club 142, 239
Alaska Territorial Mother of the Year
.... 133
Alaskan of the Year 184, 206,
.... 208, 209, 210, 211
Alberta 34

Aleut Lullaby 97, 123
Allen, Bill 208
Alyeska 190
Amara, Lucine 131
American Cancer Society 214, 216
Anchorage Arts Council 175,
.... 181, 185
Anchorage Concert Association
.... 5, 84, 115, 117, 118, 119, 120, 122,
... 134, 185, 198, 200, 204, 208, 218,
... 132
Anchorage Daily News 124,
... 127, 145, 153, 172, 201, 202, 203,
... 207, 211, 216
Anchorage Grocery Store 140
Anchorage Hotel 54, 66, 105,
.... 107, 126
Anchorage Little Theatre 112, 114,
.... 115, 116, 118, 119, 123, 134
Anchorage Mental Health Association
.... 153
Anchorage Opera 116, 124, 218

Anchorage Public School .... 62, ... 63, 64, 75, 81, 134
Anchorage Symphony .... 119, ... 174, 175, 176
Anchorage Times .... 15, 63, 78, 91, ... 96, 98, 100, 101, 104, 108, 109, 110, ... 116, 118, 121, 125, 127, 140, 142, ... 143, 169, 171, 198, 199, 200
Anchorage Welcoming Service 109
Anchorage Women's Club .... 83, ... 92, 133, 139
Anglemyer, Richard 120
Anna Lou 8
Annabell, Rusty 67
Arctic Ice Worms 62
Arctic Summeretta 116, 123
Artique 110
Atkinson, Tom 176, 178, 179
Atlantic City 154, 155, 156, 163, 173
Atwood, Evangeline 76, 124, 204
Atwood, Robert .... 15, 111, 127, 199, ... 208, 211

B

Bagoy, Eileen 64
Baker, Margaret 64
Baldwin, Charan 92
Balhizer, Marjorie 64
Balls, Alfred 92
Barber, Ed 92,
Barnes, Marion 83
Barske, Dianne 1, 2, 5
Bartlett, Bob 158, 160
Baughman, Wayne 114
Beck, Larry 157, 158, 203

Benson, Benny 86
Bernstein, Leonard 128, 130
Beta Sigma Phi . 119, 125, 126, 127, 134
Bible 19
Bitar, Robert 162
Black Bear Award 202
Bockoven, Hal 116
Bonanza Days 101, 102, 103
Bootleggers Cove 87
Bowen, Margaret 81
Bowers, William 196
Bragaw, Robert 92
Brice, Carol 121
Briggs, Ruth 171, 172
Brink, Frank 114, 123
Britch, Peter 119
Brower, John 196, 197, 218
Brown, Louise 139
Buckner, Brig General Simon B. Jr 86
Burgan, Bea 75
Business and Professional Women's Club .... 92, ... 171, 172

C

Caliban 21, 26
Callihan, Aenid 211
Callihan, Ed 211, 213
Camp Fire 20, 21, 24, 33, 34, 186
Captain Cook Hotel 170
Carey, Hilda 75
Carr, Larry 208
Carter, Virginia 188
Carter's Jewelry Store 28

Catholic 59, 115
Chamber of Commerce 92, 109,
.... 119, 134, 136, 172, 199
Chamberlain, Mrs. R.L. 119
Chei, Fred 172
Chenoweth, Kathryn 208
Chesarek, F. J. 84
Churchill, WInston 182
Claire 34
Cleaves, Irene 119
Cliburn, Van 128, 130
Coats, John 92
Cochran, Grant 113, 114
Cochran, Herb 83
Collins, John 132
Community Chorus 15, 86,
... 113, 114, 116, 119, 122, 134, 185,
.... 198, 199, 208
Comstock, Theda 145
Concert Chorus 15, 113, 196,
.... 197, 199, 208, 218
Concert Hour 98
Connor, Jerry 183, 184
Conrady, Marguerite 92
Cooper, Earl 114, 119
Cope, Alonzo 69
Cordova Airlines 166
Coutts A.W. 92
Couper, Steve Gov. 209
Crawford, Bertha 64
Cuddy, Lucy 144, 146
Cuddy,W.M. 92
Culver, Walter 94, 101
Curzi, Cesare 122

Cuthbertson, Bill 9
Cuthbertson, Don 13
Cuthbertson, Jim 9
Cuthbertson, Margaret Ellen ("Ella")
Dunlap 8, 18
Cuthbertson, Matthew 8, 18
Cuthbertson, William ALexander
.... 8, 192

D

Dash, Delores 191, 218
Davis 11, 23
DeLeon, Nancy Wellman 162
DeLong, Annette 102
Delta Kappa Gamma 172, 197, 198
DePaul, Ed 115
Depression 25, 27, 68, 70, 71, 73
Derfner, Carol 200
Designer Room 154
Desmond, Sally Sampson 179
Diamond Tooth Gertie 101
Die Fledermaus 124
Dimond, Anne 116
Dodd, Carol Anne Harrison 10, 11,
... 12, 38, 74, 75, 76, 77, 78, 81, 82, 85,
... 86, 88, 89, 90, 94, 105, 116, 133, 134,
... 135, 136, 143, 154, 162, 164, 165,166,
... 167, 168, 178, 179, 185, 215, 217
Dodd, Diane 11, 12, 134,
.... 167, 185, 216, 217
Dodd, Diane 12, 13
Dodd, Ed 11, 13, 22, 185, 207
Dodd, Jack 12
Dodd, Kari 12
Dodd, Robert 12, 88, 133, 135

Dodd, Ruth 135
Doran, Vince 212, 214
Douglass, Bill 164
Drake, Marie 86
Drykers, John 163
Dubonnet, Maurice 174,
.... 175, 178, 200
Dunkle, Billie 97
Dunlap, Harold 33
Dusenbury, Elinor 86

E

Eagan, Bill 217
Eagan, Neva 217
Earl 10, 211
Ehling, Dewey 200
Elda 8, 86
Elks 55, 62, 75, 78, 79,
.... 80, 89, 125, 126, 133
Elliott, Lenora 185
Emard Cannery 68
Emergency Housing Bureau Director ...
... 107
Emily (the dog) 127, 137,
.... 165, 166, 176, 178
Emmons, Delos C. 108
Empress Theatre 63, 76, 81
English, Flossie 24
Episcopal 115
Eroh, Charles 115
Etude Magazine 83, 84
Excelsior Springs 17

F

Fahrenbruch, Marie 35
Farell, Marita 116, 117,
.... 121, 123, 124, 135
Faris, Betty 110
Farrel, Marita 116
Faulds, Jack 119
Ficken, Ben 48
Fiedler, Arthur 122
Fildes, Kenneth 98, 101
First Lady 28, 125, 126
Fisher, Helen 100
Flora Dora Tavern 101
Florence Currier 22, 28, 33, 34
Flossie 24, 25, 26, 27
Fluffy 26
Flynn, Mary 198
Forney, Clifford 31
Fort Richardson 90, 91, 114, 115
Fousek, Blanche 75, 102
Fox, Mary Dee 156
Francis, Arlene 142, 143
Franks, Pat 187, 188
Frederick, Louise 9
Fried, Howard 163
Fromberg 32, 35, 36,
.... 37, 38, 39, 41, 45
Fur Rendezvous 79, 80,
.... 86, 90, 101, 102, 136, 156, 201

G

Gaines, Ruben 156
Gall, Alwin E. 175
Garden of Eatin 177, 178
Gay, Richard 218
Gellis, Gus 62
Golden Rule Foundation 134
Goodman, Norma 172, 173

Gottstein, J.B. 92
Grady, Gladys 119
Grandma Hat 11, 155, 207
Greater Anchorage Chamber of Commerce 172
Greater Anchorage, Inc. 153
Green, Perry 208
GRIT Magazine 185
Grizzell, Florence 33

H

Haines, Marilyn 134
Hale, George 145
Hale, Mary 114, 145
Hallelujah Chorus 218
Hammond, Jay 208
Hansel and Gretel 124
Hanshew, U.S. 92
Harlacher, Betty 75
Harrison, Eric 10, 185
Harrison, Jack 66, 67, 69,
.... 81, 86, 91, 92, 96,
.... 101, 104, 108, 118,
.... 119, 121, 122, 125, 127, 145
Hasher 41
Hat Chats 145
Hatfield, Lansing 117
Haycroft, Jane 173
Heitmeyers, Dr. 79
Heginbotham, Lois 32
Hermanson, Jeff 12
Heston, Charlton 114
Hewitt, Nell 62, 66
Hickel, Walter 163, 170, 185, 208
Hildeman, Erma 27, 190

Hommon, Dorothy 161
Hommon, Karol 160, 161
Hopper, Hedda 97, 100, 173
Horne, Marilyn 128
Hostess House 173
Hurst, James 119
Hurst, Ruth 102
Hyde, A. 27

J

Jackson, George 119
Jensen, Paul 173, 174
Johannesen, Grant 116, 121
Johansen, Pettit Colleen 156, 157
John Robert Powers Finishing School and Modeling School 216
Johnson, Art 123
Johnson, Lyndon B. 158. 160
Jones, Vanny 62
Junior Theater Guild 87

K

Kanazawa, Tomiko 122
Karstens, Harry P. 58
KBYR 111, 124
Kelli 11, 12
KENI 118, 139
Kennedy, Jackie 142
KFIA 136, 140
KFQD 55, 62, 84, 87, 156
Kilbourn, Eleanor 29
Killeen, Donna 134
Kimura, Sammy 90
Kinsell, Bill 75
Kirchner, Gerry 135
Kirchner, Hans 176, 177

Kirkpatrick, Mildred 75
Kiwanis 119
Knapp, Forrest 91
Knowles, Tony 209
Kroesing, Diane 134
Kruger, Betty 64
KTVA 173
Kuhns, Diana 217

L

Lally, Hank 75
Lamoreaux, Russ 134
Larson, Emily 217
Laurence, Jeanne 125, 126
Laurence, Jeannie 80
Laurence, Sydney 54, 80, 133
Learned, Marjorie 126
Lee, Bessie 71
Leer, Charlotte 75
Lehman, Lois 45, 47
Lesh, Keith 119
Lestock, Lewis 171
Limonick, Natalie 138
Lindgren, Bill 177
Linton, Kay 208
Lions Club 107
Lishner, Leon 163
Liska, Erma 190, 191
Little Symphony Orchestra 116
Livingston, Martin 123
Lorene's Scrapbook 4, 136,
.... 139, 140, 141
Loughlin, Ken 76
Loussac, Z. J. 142
Lutheran 59, 115

M

Magic Voice 21
Marcus, Bruce 114
Marton, Myrtle 64
Matthews, Bertha 23
McCreery, Ruth 122
McGarey, Marjorie 21, 22, 23
McKean, Ethel 28
McKee, Mabel 31, 34, 41
Melton, Bard 139
Menaker, Steven 196
Merrill, Russ 69
Merrill, Russell 65
Messiah 82, 83, 113,
.... 115, 116, 218
Methodist 122, 161
Mills, Agnes 75
Minowe 21
Miss Alaska 154, 155, 156,
... 157, 159, 160, 161, 162, 163, 164,
... 170, 173, 176, 178, 199, 201, 218
Miss Alaska Centennial 157,
.... 159, 160, 164
Miss America Pagent 154, 160,
.... 161, 173, 199
Morton, Carl 135
Morton, Nell Mary 135
Mother of the arts 15, 200, 208, 211
Mulcahy, Gertrude 87
Mumford, George 110, 135
Murray, Billy 61, 63
Musical Courier 83, 84

N

New Testament 19

Nidiffer, Mary Ruth 161, 170
Niemi, Rica 49, 67, 68, 78, 211
Nixon, Richard, President 216
Norquist, Royal 114

O

O'Connor, George 38
Old Testament 19
Oliver, Simeon 96, 97, 123
Ollerinshaw, Marion 61
Ormandy, Eugene 128, 132
Ortland, Davis 12
Ortland, Remy 12
Ortland, Romney 12, 13
Ortland, Stephen 12
Ortland, Tanner 12
Our Town 114

P

Pantages Circuit 55
Paratore, Anthony 5, 119
Paratore, Joseph 5, 119
Penguin Club 145
Performing Arts Center 62, 73, 89,
... 197, 202, 204, 218
Perman, Ira 119, 120, 200, 208
Peterson, Elsie 64
Petroleum Wives Club 145
Pettit, Colleen 156, 157,
.... 159, 160, 164
Phillips, Brad 143, 144, 145, 146, 147
Pillow Puncher 41
Pioneers' Home 4, 16, 29,
... 49, 89, 128, 187, 188, 201, 205, 211,
... 212, 213, 215, 216, 217
Pirates of Penzance 124

Plowman, Earlene 163
Polk, Bob 43
Pollock, Howard 158, 160
Pond, Bob 112, 114
Popper, Jan 138
Porter, Viola 89
Presbyterian 18, 41, 59, 76, 78,
... 81, 83, 84, 86, 90, 92, 96, 100, 115,
... 122, 123, 125, 127, 134, 135, 136,
... 145, 175, 187, 189, 207, 208, 212
Prichard, Marie 35
Priem, Wayne 75
Purnell, Doc 124

R

Raja and Shala 133
Rasmuson, Elmer 7, 172
Reer, Fran Sr. 208
Reed, Mrs. Frank L. 79
Remy 11
Renner, Laura 217
Reo 27
Rex, Ratta 25
Richards, Charles 102
Robert's Rules of Order 18
Robinson, Alyce 168, 171, 183
Roger, Louis 213, 214, 215
Rogers, Calvin 114
Rogers, Ginger 97, 100
Romeros 131
Romney 9, 11, 12, 185
Rosenthal, Paul 218
Rosvold, Irving 104, 105
Rotary Club 119
Rullman, Jayne 84

S

Savola, Anna 64
Schapiro, Maxim 115, 116,
.... 117, 120, 121, 122, 124
Schriner, Ralph 96
Seattle Post-Intelligencer 122
Seattle Symphony 122
See, A. B. 114
Sermon on the Mount 27, 28
Shakespeare 66
Sharon 10, 211
Sharp, Maurice 61, 79
Sharrock, George 172
Shawn 11
Silva, Luigi 117
Simonds, Cleo 75
Slade, Mary Lou 75
Sly, Cecil 45, 46, 63, 64
Smart, Gary 175
Smart Shop 110
Smith College 161
Smith, Opal Lu 119
Smith, Selma 146, 150
Smith, W.A. 92
Snight, Elly 75
Snight, Peggy 75
Sogn, Elsie 76
Soroptimist 119, 134, 145
Sourdough Sentinel 103
Stang, Gordon 134
Stapleton, Rob 208
Sterling 8, 16, 17, 18, 19,
... 20, 21, 22, 25, 26, 29, 31, 32, 41,
... 45, 46, 47, 48, 54, 57, 59, 61, 68,
... 70, 98, 103, 104, 185, 186, 187, 190,
... 200, 201, 202
Sterling College 17, 22, 30,
.... 31, 32, 37, 45, 202
Stern, Isaac 128
Stoddard, Vivian 64
Straight, Willard 163, 164
Stubrud, Tracey 13
Suddock, Fran 218
Sullivan, George 197, 198, 208
Swank, Gladys 135
Swanson, Rica 49, 78, 211

T

Tanner 11
Telder, Clarice 75
The Hat Box 5, 110, 111,
... 112, 122, 123, 128, 134, 139, 145,
... 153, 154, 161, 164, 165, 169, 170,
... 171, 173, 175, 184, 187, 215, 216
The Hat Box Rag 175
Thomas, Lowell 181
Thomas, Willard 119
Tobin, William J. 7, 208
Totenberg, Roman 117
Toyon of Alaska 163, 164
Tyrell, J.T. 45

U

USO 7, 91, 92, 93, 94,
... 95, 96, 97, 98, 100, 101, 102, 103,
... 104, 107, 108, 114

V

Vaara, Mabel 126
Vagabond King 124
Vail, Farrel 200

Veilbig, Earl 11
Veilbig, Eric H. 11
Vielbig, Joseph 11, 87,
.... 133, 134, 211
Vielbig, Klindt 134
Veilbig, Melody 11
Vielbig, Pegge Lee Harrison 10,
... 11, 68, 70, 71, 73, 74, 77, 78, 80,
... 81, 82, 85, 86, 87, 89,
... 90, 94, 105, 116, 133, 134, 154, 164
... 185, 200, 201, 211, 218
Veilbig, Sharon 11
Veilbig, Steven 11
Voth, Elvera 200, 209

W

Wade, Ruthella 116
Wagner, Bill 62
Waldorf Astoria 123
Walker, Eleanor 28
Walker, S.L. 185, 186
Walkowski, Dodi 122
Wallulus, Charlie 107
Warber, Paul 119
Waring, Fred 128
Warriner, Georgia 75
Watt, Emili 12
Watt, Kelli Dodd 12, 13
Watt, Paul 12
Watt, Shawn 12
Welches 110
Welling, Charmaine 195
Wellman De Leon 218
Wellman, Nancy 162, 163, 218
Wennerstrom, Bert 62

Westmark Hotel 77, 78, 91
Westward Hotel 111, 153,
.... 169, 170, 171, 177
Wilkins, Bob 120, 124
Wilkins, Robert 118, 196, 200
Williams, Walter 210, 213
Willis, Jeannie 186, 188
Wilma 34
Wood, Ross 181
Wood, William 208
Works, Doris (Mrs. R. L.) 79
World War I 27, 36, 67
World War II 90, 215
Wyatt, Anna Lou 9
Wyatt, Bill 9, 134
Wyatt, Bob 9, 86
Wyatt, Dick 9
Wyatt, Elda 9
Wyatt, Fran 9
Wyatt, Nina 8, 13, 17, 20,
... 26, 34, 48, 87, 138, 185, 186, 187

Y

Yellowstone 39, 41, 42,
.... 43, 45, 46, 47, 62
You Name It 95, 96, 97

Z

Ziegler, Eustice 105